CONTENTS

BRIGHTRED STUDY GUIDE: NATIONAL 5 FRENCH

SOCIETY

LEARNING

EMPLOYABILITY

CULTURE

COURSE ASSESSMENT: WRITING

COURSE ASSESSMENT

GLOSSARY

INTRODUCING NATIONAL 5 FRENCH

During this course you will further develop your linguistic knowledge and apply skills for learning, for life and for work purposes.

Learning any language will help you to develop your literacy skills both in the foreign language and English, and improve your cultural knowledge about other countries.

THE NATIONAL 5 FRENCH COURSE

National 5 French encourages you to become a more confident learner; a responsible citizen with an informed and ethical view of other cultures and traditions in Francophone countries; someone who can work independently as well as participate in group discussions and team work.

UNIT ASSESSMENTS AND EXTERNAL ASSESSMENT

What does National 5 involve?

To gain the full award at National 5, you will need to pass all of the Unit assessments as well as the Course assessment (external exam). As you work through this course you will enhance your vocabulary, develop skills in listening, reading and writing, and apply knowledge about language to help improve accuracy. This will give you the confidence to both pass the Unit assessment and feel fully prepared for your examination.

The skills that you develop during your National 5 course will be assessed in two ways:

1   Unit assessments in reading/writing, listening and talking

2   A Course assessment in reading/writing, listening and talking (Performance).

Unit assessments are not graded – they are internally assessed on a pass or fail basis. The Course assessment is graded A–D and, with the exception of the Performance assessment, these are graded by SQA.

PUTTING THE FOUR SKILLS TO THE TEST

Throughout the year you will be assessed on the four skills of reading, writing, listening and talking. The two units you will need to complete are called Understanding Language (National 5) and Using Language (National 5).

The vocabulary which you cover in class and which is then assessed in your Unit assessments covers the four contexts: society, learning, employability and culture. This book will take you through each of these contexts, exploring all of the useful vocabulary that will come up in your Unit assessments and in the exam.

ONLINE

The SQA website gives more detail on the grammar and topics that you will need to know about. Follow the link from www.brightredbooks. net/N5French

ONLINE

This book is supported by the BrightRED Digital Zone. Log in at www. brightredbooks.net/N5French to unlock a world of videos, links, tests and much more!

DON'T FORGET

Whilst covering the context and topics in each chapter, you will develop your language skills, increase your vocabulary and be given the opportunity to revise grammatical structures. After each topic you will be asked to use the language learned to write a short essay about the topic. This should help you to consolidate the language learned and you may also wish to use these essays to help prepare your Performance (talking) as part of the external examination.

UNIT ASSESSMENTS: THE FOUR SKILLS ASSESSED

The Unit assessments you complete must prove your ability in reading, writing, listening and talking.

Talking	Listening	Reading	Writing
This means proving that you can deliver a presentation, have a conversation, ask and answer questions, take part in a role-play, produce an oral summary of something you have heard or read, give opinions, etc. You will be assessed on the complexity of the vocabulary and structures you use, the accuracy of your language, your pronunciation, your ability to speak fluently and your understanding of what is said by the other person in the conversation.	Here you will have to prove that you can understand statements made in French. You will have to listen to extracts in French and then answer questions in English on what you've heard, or produce a summary.	This involves testing your ability to understand texts. You will be assessed on this in various ways, for example you may have to answer questions on, or produce a summary of, a text.	This means showing your ability to produce accurate and complex pieces of writing in French on various topics and in various styles. You will be assessed on accuracy, content, structure and level of language, and the variation and complexity of your structures and vocabulary.

You will need to complete one assessment within each of the skills of reading, writing, listening and talking to fulfil the two Outcomes of the two units: Understanding Language and Using Language. The assessment approach may differ depending on your teacher/lecturer and your individual needs and interests. You may do an assessment on each individual skill or a combined assessment in which two skills are assessed.

HOW THIS BOOK CAN HELP YOU

BrightRED Study Guide: National 5 French focuses on your work in the year leading up to the examination. It offers you a study 'toolkit' containing: topic-by-topic revision of the National 5 course; progression through contexts and suggested topics; development of language skills; effective techniques for handling exam questions and a range of ways to revise, either on your own or with friends.

Chapter 1: Society	Chapter 2: Learning	Chapter 3: Employability	Chapter 4: Culture	Chapter 5: Writing
Society covers the language needed to discuss relationships with family and friends; healthy lifestyles and illnesses related to a unhealthy lifestyle; media and the impact of reality shows and new technology on our lives; citizenship and the importance of learning foreign languages; the environment and the differences between town and country life and your local area as a tourist centre.	Learning covers the language needed to discuss education and exam preparation; different education systems and responsibilities of learners.	Employability covers the language needed to discuss different jobs, including part-time work; cover letters, CVs and job applications and reviewing achievements and evaluating experiences.	Culture covers the language needed to discuss your best holiday/trip; the importance of travelling; aspects of other countries, including special events and occasions and literature/films.	Writing covers the language you will need to allow you to feel fully prepared for the Writing paper in the exam. This includes personal details (name, age, where you live); school/college education experience until now; skills/interests you have which make you right for the job; related work experience and possible examples of the two unpredictable bullet points.

BEYOND THE EXAM

Not only will this book help you to prepare for and do well in National 5 French, it will also help lay down the skills you will need to do well next year if you decide to continue with Higher French or study a new foreign language at Higher or National 5, take Modern Languages for Work Purposes Units, go into further study or training, or simply continue into the world of work.

 DON'T FORGET

It is now up to you. We hope this book will prove useful and help prepare you fully for both the Unit and Course assessments. Bonne chance!

SOCIETY

FAMILY AND FRIENDS – LA FAMILLE ET LES AMIS 1

The Society context can cover a wide range of topics. We will look at each topic in turn within this context and develop your 'toolkit' of language skills, knowledge of vocabulary and grammar. The themes will include:

- relationships with family and friends
- conflicts at home
- healthy lifestyles
- lifestyle-related illnesses
- media

- technology
- life in town compared to life in the countryside
- your home area as a tourist centre
- environment.

LET'S GET STARTED!

Let's start with the subject of family and friends. Can you think of what you would like to be able to say about your relationships with your family and friends?

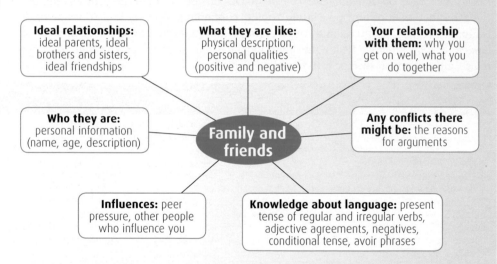

Ideal relationships: ideal parents, ideal brothers and sisters, ideal friendships

What they are like: physical description, personal qualities (positive and negative)

Your relationship with them: why you get on well, what you do together

Who they are: personal information (name, age, description)

Family and friends

Any conflicts there might be: the reasons for arguments

Influences: peer pressure, other people who influence you

Knowledge about language: present tense of regular and irregular verbs, adjective agreements, negatives, conditional tense, avoir phrases

YOUR FAMILY AND FRIENDS, WHO ARE THEY? – TA FAMILLE ET TES AMIS, C'EST QUI?

Quiz

Can you remember the vocabulary in French for the following?

- Members of the family
- What he or she is called
- What age someone is (don't forget to use *avoir* for age!)
- Numbers, days and months
- When someone's birthday is

DON'T FORGET

This is a perfect opportunity to revise vocabulary that you have previously learned.

THE PRESENT TENSE – LE PRÉSENT

When talking about your family relationships, you will mostly use the **present tense**. There are **regular** and **irregular verbs** that you will need to know. Take the following steps to form regular verbs:

1. Write down the subject (the person or thing doing the verb).

2. Write down the **infinitive** without the 'er', 'ir' or 're' ending (this is known as the stem of the **verb**).

3. Add the present tense ending (this must correspond to the subject).

> **EXAMPLE**
>
> *Jouer* – to play (this is known as the infinitive)
> Chop off the 'er' to form the stem: *jou*
> Write down the subject and the root and add the correct 'er' verb ending: I play
> – *Je jou**e***

ONLINE TEST

Take the test 'Can you remember all the endings for regular 'er', 'ir' and 're' verbs?' at www.brightredbooks.net/ N5French

VIDEO LINK

Check out the clip 'Avec la famille' at www. brightredbooks.net/N5French

IRREGULAR VERBS – LES VERBES IRRÉGULIERS

Let's move on to irregular verbs. You need to know these off by heart as they do not follow a pattern. The most important ones that you must learn are:

avoir – to have	vouloir – to want to	partir – to leave
être – to be	pouvoir – to be able to/can	sortir – to go out
aller – to go	devoir – to have to/must	
faire – to do/make	savoir – to know how to	

THINGS TO DO AND THINK ABOUT

Now that you are a 'present tense expert', make up 12 sentences using the present tense. Include the following verbs in your sentences:

a regular 'er' verb	faire
a regular 'ir' verb	vouloir
a regular 're' verb	pouvoir
avoir	devoir
être	partir
aller	sortir

FAMILY AND FRIENDS – LA FAMILLE ET LES AMIS 2

DON'T FORGET

When describing someone, remember that **adjectives** in French must agree! If the **noun** that you are describing is masculine plural, you must add 's' to the end of the adjective. If the noun is feminine singular, add 'e' to the end of the adjective and if the noun is feminine plural, add 'es' to the end of the adjective. Use your dictionary to check the gender of nouns if you are unsure.

DON'T FORGET

It might be an idea to revise the verb être here as you will need to know it to describe what someone's personality is like.

LISTENING

Audio tracks to support these activities are available free at www. brightredpublishing.co.uk. If you would prefer to use a CD, contact us at info@ brightredpublishing.co.uk

DON'T FORGET

A **false friend** is a word in French that looks like a word in English but means something different, for example you might guess that *sympathique* means 'sympathetic' as it looks similar, but it actually means 'nice'.

WHAT IS HE/SHE LIKE? – COMMENT EST-IL/ELLE?

You might want to describe what members of your family or your friends look like. Try to think back to when you learned to describe someone's height, hair and eyes.

> **EXAMPLE**
>
> Ma mère est petite, ma sœur a les cheveux noirs.

It is also useful to be able to describe what someone's personality is like. Let's start with the positives.

Learning vocabulary

Firstly, read through the following adjectives and cover up the English meanings. If you know some words already, put a tick or a green mark beside these words. If there are some words that you think you could guess because they look like English words, put a dash or an orange mark beside these words. Be careful, some of them might be **false friends**!

If there are some words that you don't recognise, put a cross or a red mark beside these words and, when doing your revision, spend more time going over and learning these words.

You can listen to these adjectives online to help you with the pronunciation.

Positive adjective	English meaning
aimable	pleasant
amusant(e)	fun
bavard(e)	chatty
compréhenif(-ive)	understanding
disponible	available
doux(-ce)	gentle
drôle	funny
généreux(-euse)	generous
gentil(le)	nice, kind
intelligent(e)	intelligent
ouvert(e)	open
patient(e)	patient
plein(e) de vie	full of life
rigolo(te)	funny
sage	sensible
sensible	sensitive
vif(-ve)	lively

⚙ ACTIVITY: NEGATIVES – LES NÉGATIFS

You can use any of these **adjectives** in a negative sentence. All you need to do is put *ne* before the verb (this changes to *n'* if the verb begins with a vowel or a silent 'h') and put the negative word (pas) after the verb.

Here is a reminder of some useful **negatives**. Translate the following sentences and then try to make up five phrases using negative constructions and positive adjectives.

Ne ... pas – not
Mon frère aîné n'est pas patient.

contd

Ne ... jamais – never
Ma mère n'est jamais vive.

Ne ... plus – not any more
Mon père n'est plus casse-pieds, il m'écoute.

Ne ... que – only
Ma sœur cadette n'est amusante qu'avec ses amis.

Ne ... personne – no-one
Personne n'est compréhensif chez moi.

Ne ... rien – nothing
Ma sœur aînée n'est pas généreuse, elle ne me donne rien.

⚙ ACTIVITY: NEGATIVE ADJECTIVES – LES ADJECTIFS NÉGATIFS

Once you feel confident with these phrases, move on to the negative adjectives.

Negative adjective	English meaning
antipathique	unpleasant
arrogant(e)	arrogant
autoritaire	bossy
bête	stupid
casse-pieds	annoying
démodé(e)	old-fashioned
égoïste	selfish
embêtant(e)	annoying
ennuyeux(-euse)	boring
fainéant(e)	lazy
gâté(e)	spoilt
grincheux(-euse)	grumpy
impatient(e)	impatient
irritant(e)	irritating
méchant(e)	mean
paresseux(-euse)	lazy
pénible	a nuisance
puéril(e)	childish
sévère	strict

You might like to add some **qualifiers/intensifiers**:

assez – quite	vraiment – really
un peu – a bit	trop – too
très – very	

ONLINE TEST

Take the 'Negative and positive adjectives' test online at www.brightredbooks.net/N5French.

▶ **VIDEO LINK**

Watch the 'Family and relationships' clip at www.brightredbooks.net/N5French

THINGS TO DO AND THINK ABOUT

Write a paragraph about the members of your family and include names, ages, birthdays and physical descriptions. This could be used as part of your Performance and it is worthwhile revision.

Write a second paragraph about what each member of your family is like. Don't forget to use negatives and qualifiers in your writing.

RELATIONSHIPS – LES RELATIONS

Think about why you get on well with members of your family or friends and why you sometimes argue with them. It would be useful to learn these important phrases to help you describe your relationships.

POSITIVE RELATIONSHIPS – LES RAPPORTS POSITIFS

- J'ai une bonne relation avec … – I have a good relationship with …
- J'ai un bon rapport avec … – I have a good relationship with …
- Je m'entends bien avec … – I get on well with …
- Je me sens proche de … – I feel close to …

It is useful to be able to say why you get on well with family members and friends. Here are some phrases to help:

- … car/parce que/ parce qu'…
- mon père/ma mère/ mon frère/ma sœur est + positive adjective
- il/elle est + adjective

DON'T FORGET

When listening to and reading French text, try to make links with words in English in order to work out the meaning of unfamiliar vocabulary, for example *intérêts* looks like 'interests'. By listening to and reading a text, you can also prepare your pronunciation.

ACTIVITY: POSITIVE RELATIONSHIPS – LES RAPPORTS POSITIFS

Read the following French phrases and match them to the English meanings. You can listen to these phrases online to help you with pronunciation.

on s'intéresse aux mêmes choses	we spend a lot of time together
on partage les mêmes intérêts	he/she is very respectful of my private life
on a beaucoup de choses en commun	he/she respects me
il/elle a un bon sens de l'humour	we share the same interests
on passe beaucoup de temps ensemble	he/she supports me when I have a problem
on fait tout ensemble	he/she is always in a good mood

contd

on sort souvent ensemble	he/she helps me when I need it
on partage de bons moments	we can discuss everything
il/elle est toujours de bonne humeur	we do everything together
on rigole	we are interested in the same things
on peut discuter de tout	we have a lot of things in common
il/elle me respecte	we share good times together
on est très proche	we often go out together
il/elle est très respectueux(-euse) de ma vie privée	we have a laugh
il/elle m'aide quand j'en ai besoin	he/she has a good sense of humour
il/elle me soutient quand j'ai un problème	we are very close

DON'T FORGET

You must check adjective agreements, see page 8, for example *mon frère est rigolo/ma soeur est rigolote.*

⚙ ACTIVITY: PARENTAL RELATIONSHIPS – LES RELATIONS AVEC SES PARENTS

Read the text below first and look up any words you don't know in the dictionary. Then try to predict what you might hear and think of any French vocabulary that could be used to fill the gaps and complete the sentences.

Then listen to the audio track to hear people talking about the relationships they have with their parents. Fill in the gaps then translate the phrases into English.

1. Mes parents me laissent _____ avec mes ____ tous les week-ends.

2. Mes parents me laissent assez de _____.

3. Mes parents me _____ beaucoup d'argent de ____.

4. Mes parents sont très _____ de ma vie _____.

5. Je _____ très bien avec mes parents car ils me font _____.

6. Mes parents sont très _____ et ils me donnent de bons _____.

7. Je suis très _____ de mes parents car on peut _____ de tout.

8. J'ai de la chance car je _____ dc tout avec mes parents et on _____ aux mêmes choses.

9. Ma mère est toujours de bonne _____ et on _____ cnsemble.

compréhensifs	donnent	rigole	discuter	conseils	respectueux
liberté	poche	sortir	discute	humeur	confiance
proche	amis	m'entends	s'intéresse	privée	

ONLINE TEST

Take the test 'Relationships – Les relations' at www.brightredbooks.net/N5French.

VIDEO LINK

Check out the clip 'Family and marriage' at www.brightredbooks.net/N5French

⚠ THINGS TO DO AND THINK ABOUT

Adapt any phrases that you like about positive family relationships and write a paragraph to describe your relationships with people in your family. You may wish to learn this paragraph for your Performance.

FAMILY CONFLICTS – LES CONFLITS FAMILIAUX 1

Although we may get on well with our families, there can be arguments from time to time. What do you tend to argue about with your parents, brothers and sisters? To introduce family conflicts, you may want to start by saying that you don't get on well with someone in particular and then give reasons why. Here are a few ideas.

 ACTIVITY: NEGATIVE RELATIONSHIPS 1 – LES RAPPORTS NÉGATIFS 1

Listen to the audio track to hear how these phrases are pronounced then translate them into English.

1. J'ai une mauvaise relation avec ma sœur.
2. J'ai un mauvais rapport avec ma grand-mère.
3. Je m'entends mal avec mon oncle.
4. Je ne m'entends pas bien avec mon frère.
5. Je me dispute souvent avec mes parents.
6. De temps en temps, il y a des tensions avec mes parents.

DON'T FORGET

You can use adverbs of frequency to emphasise how often you argue with your family.

 ACTIVITY: ADVERBS – LES ADVERBES

Can you work out what these words mean? Use the percentages in brackets as a clue to help you.

1. Toujours (100%)
2. Souvent (70%)
3. Parfois/quelquefois (40%)
4. De temps en temps (30%)
5. Rarement (10%)

Here are some examples of these words in use. Can you work out what the rule is for where to place these **adverbs** of frequency?

1. Je me dispute souvent avec mon frère.
2. On se dispute toujours.
3. Je me dispute parfois avec mon père.
4. On se dispute de temps en temps.
5. Je me dispute rarement avec ma mère.

ONLINE TEST

Take the test 'Family conflicts – Les conflits de la famille' at www.brightredbooks.net/N5French.

 ACTIVITY: NEGATIVE RELATIONSHIPS 2 – LES RAPPORTS NÉGATIFS 2

Here are some reasons why there may be conflicts or tensions with your family or friends.

Can you work out what they mean?

Je me dispute avec mes parents/mon père/ma mère/mon frère/ma sœur car/parce que/parce qu'...

1. mon père/ma mère/mon frère/ma soeur est + negative adjective.
2. mes parents sont + adjective (*don't forget agreement!*).
3. il/elle est + negative adjective.
4. ils sont + negative adjective (*don't forget agreement!*).
5. il/elle prend mes vêtements sans me demander la permission.

VIDEO LINK

Watch 'Children and their parents' at www.brightredbooks.net/N5French

contd

6. il/elle ment tout le temps.
7. mes parents veulent regarder des émissions différentes à la télé.
8. il/elle écoute de la musique trop fort quand je fais mes devoirs.
9. il/elle change son comportement devant mes parents.
10. mon père se moque de moi devant mes amis.
11. mes frères me taquinent tout le temps.
12. ma sœur utilise mon maquillage/mon ordinateur sans me demander la permission.

ARGUMENTS – LES DISPUTES

You might want to be more specific about the arguments that you have with your parents. You can start by talking about general reasons for arguments and then go into more detail. When talking about arguments with your parents, make sure you use the third person plural endings (ils).

THINGS TO DO AND THINK ABOUT

Read the following sentences and work out what they mean. Try to find links between English and French vocabulary to help you work out what the vocabulary means before checking in the dictionary.

Listen to the phrases online to help you with pronunciation.

Je me dispute avec mes parents à cause ...

... des études
- Ils pensent que je n'étudie pas assez.
- Ils ne sont pas contents de mes notes au lycée.

... des sorties
- Ils ne me laissent pas sortir avec mes amis pendant la semaine.
- Ils ne me laissent pas assez de liberté.

... de mes amis
... de mon petit ami/ma petite amie
- Ils n'aiment pas mes amis/mon petit ami/ma petite amie.
- Ils pensent que je passe trop de temps avec mes amis.
- Ils croient que je suis trop jeune pour avoir un petit ami/une petite amie.

... de l'argent
- Ils ne me donnent pas assez d'argent.
- Ils pensent que je gaspille mon argent.
- Ils ne me laissent pas trouver un petit boulot pour gagner de l'argent.

... des tâches ménagères
- Ils pensent que je ne fais rien à la maison et que je suis trop paresseux (-euse).
- Je crois que j'aide beaucoup à la maison mais ils ne sont pas d'accord.
- Je dois faire beaucoup de ménage mais mon frère ne fait rien.

... ma vie privée
- Ils se mêlent de mes affaires.
- Ils ne respectent pas ma vie privée.
- Ils veulent toujours savoir ce qui se passe dans ma vie, ce qui m'énerve.
- Ils posent trop de questions de mes amis/de mon petit copain/de ma petite copine/de mes études.

... de mon comportement
- Ils pensent que je suis désobéissant(e).
- Ils ne sont pas contents de mon comportement à la maison/l'école.

... de mes passe-temps
- Ils pensent que je passe trop de temps à regarder la télé/écouter de la musique/jouer à l'ordinateur.

- Ils disent que je passe trop de temps sur internet/sur mon portable/sur Facebook.

DON'T FORGET
Can you spot how the verbs change when the subject/person changes from singular to plural? Look back at the present tense summary at the start of this unit to revise how the endings change.

DON'T FORGET
The infinitive is the name of the verb which ends in 'er', 'ir' or 're' in French and in English, it is when we put 'to' in front of the verb, for example *regarder* – to watch.

ONLINE TEST
Head to the BrightRED Digital Zone to revise endings.

FAMILY CONFLICTS- LES CONFLITS FAMILIAUX 2

ACTIVITY: ARGUMENTS WITH PARENTS 1 – LES DISPUTES AVEC SES PARENTS 1

Read the following texts about why some young people argue with their parents. Try to identify some of the vocabulary we have already covered.

For each text take notes on the following:

1. Who do they not get on with/argue with?

2. Why?

Jérôme

Malheureusement, je dirais que j'ai une mauvaise relation avec mon père. Il est toujours sur mon dos. Ça m'arrive de me disputer assez souvent avec lui. Il n'est jamais content car il pense que je passe trop de temps sur mon portable. Ce qu'il ne comprend pas, c'est que je veux parler à ma petite amie et le problème, c'est qu'il n'aime pas ma petite amie. Il croit que je suis trop jeune pour avoir une petite amie et que je devrais passer plus de temps à étudier. Ce qui m'énerve, c'est qu'il se mêle de mes affaires et à mon avis, il doit respecter ma vie privée.

Marianne

Parfois il y a des conflits chez moi à cause des tâches ménagères et de l'argent de poche. Ma mère me critique tout le temps et elle me gronde si je ne fais pas la vaisselle ou si je ne passe pas l'aspirateur. Après avoir passé une longue journée au lycée, je n'ai pas envie de faire le ménage. Ce n'est pas juste car mon frère ne fait rien à la maison. En plus, tous mes amis reçoivent vingt Euros chaque semaine de leurs parents sans aider chez eux. Ma mère ne me donnerait rien si je ne faisais pas le ménage, ce que je trouve embêtant. Je ne reçois que dix Euros chaque semaine et ça ne me suffit pas.

Put your answers into the table:

	Jérôme	Marianne
Who does he/she argue with?		
Why?		

⚙ ACTIVITY: ARGUMENTS WITH PARENTS 2 – LES DISPUTES AVEC SES PARENTS 2

Now try to put together some sentences about the arguments you have with your parents.

Here are some 'starters':

- Ça m'arrive souvent de me disputer avec mes parents à cause de ... – I often argue with my parents about ...

- Il y a des tensions avec mes parents à cause de ... – There are tensions with my parents because of ...

- À l'égard des conflits chez moi, il y a des disputes à cause de ... – With regards to conflicts at home, there are arguments about ...

- Ce qui m'énerve, c'est qu'il y a des conflits chez moi à cause de ... – What annoys me is that there are conflicts at home because of ...

- Ce que je déteste, ce sont les tensions chez moi à cause de ... – What I hate are the tensions at home because of ...

- Je dirais qu'il y a souvent des conflits chez moi à cause de ... – I would say that there are often arguments at home because of ...

DON'T FORGET

Remember, you can adapt and use these phrases in your Performance about your family relationships.

ONLINE TEST

Take the test 'Family conflicts – Les conflits familiaux' at www.brightredbooks.net/N5French

VIDEO LINK

For more, watch the clip 'La famille' at www.brightredbooks.net/N5French

THINGS TO DO AND THINK ABOUT

Write a paragraph about any arguments or tensions in your family. You may wish to use this as part of your Performance.

IDEAL PARENTS – LES PARENTS IDÉAUX

We have talked about reasons why you don't get along with your parents. We will now look at how you would describe your ideal parents. You can recycle some of the language we have already learned in this unit. You will also need to know the **conditional tense**.

- What would be your idea of a perfect parent? What would they be like?
- What would they do and what would they not do?

CONDITIONAL TENSE – LE CONDITIONNEL

You will need to know the conditional tense in order to describe your ideal parents. The conditional tense describes what someone *would* be like or what they *would* do. It is really easy to form as the endings remain the same for 'er', 'ir' and 're' verbs, although there are some irregular conditional stems that you will need to learn.

1. First write down the subject (person who is doing the verb): *Je*.

2. Then write down the infinitive: *Je jouer*.

3. Now add the conditional endings to the infinitive *Je jouerais* – I would play (although take off the 'e' at the end of 're' verbs before adding the endings, e.g. *Je prendrais* – I would take.)

The conditional endings are:

je	-ais	nous	-ions
tu	-ais	vous	-iez
il/elle/on	-ait	ils/elles	-aient

The key irregular conditional verbs that you need to know include:

- avoir – j'aurais (I would have)
- être – je serais (I would be)
- faire – je ferais (I would do/make)
- aller – j'irais (I would go)
- vouloir – je voudrais (I would like)
- pouvoir – je pourrais (I would be able to/could)
- devoir – je devrais (I would have to/should)

ACTIVITY: CONDITIONAL TENSE – LE CONDITIONNEL

Try to translate the following sentences using the conditional tense:

1. I would watch TV with my dad.
2. I would finish my homework.
3. I would read a book.
4. We would spend more time together.
5. We would talk more often.

ACTIVITY: IRREGULAR CONDITIONAL STEMS – LES VERBES IRRÉGULIERS AU CONDITIONNEL

Translate the following sentences into French using irregular conditional verbs:

1. I would go to the cinema at the weekend with my mum.
2. My dad would be more patient.
3. My parents would have more free time.
4. I would do sport with my dad.
5. I would be able to go out with my friends during the week.

AN IDEAL PARENT – UN PARENT IDÉAL

Let's start by describing the qualities of an ideal parent: we could use some negatives here as well. Have a look back at the section on negatives (page 8) if you need to revise them again.

ACTIVITY: AN IDEAL PARENT 1 – UN PARENT IDÉAL 1

Listen to the audio track and read the following phrases. Put the phrases in the correct order and translate them into English.

1. Un parent idéal laisserait assez de liberté à ses enfants.
2. Un parent idéal ne s'énerverait pas facilement.
3. Un parent idéal protègerait ses enfants.
4. Un parent idéal ne serait pas trop protecteur.
5. Un parent idéal serait patient et tolérant.
6. Un parent idéal ne serait pas démodé.
7. Un parent idéal serait toujours disponible pour aider ses enfants.
8. Un parent idéal passerait beaucoup de temps avec ses enfants.
9. Un parent idéal donnerait de bons conseils à ses enfants.
10. Un parent idéal ne gâterait jamais ses enfants.
11. Un parent idéal ferait confiance à ses enfants.

ACTIVITY: AN IDEAL PARENT 2 – UN PARENT IDÉAL 2

Now it's your turn. Choose five phrases that describe positive relationships and five phrases that describe negative relationships with parents and change them into the conditional tense to describe an ideal parent. A couple of examples have been done for you:

1. Il/elle a un bon sens de l'humour – Un parent idéal aurait un bon sens de l'humour.
2. Il/elle se moque de moi devant mes amis – Un parent idéal ne se moquerait pas de ses enfants.

THINGS TO DO AND THINK ABOUT

Write a paragraph about an ideal parent/ideal parents. You may wish to learn this as part of your Performance.

 ONLINE TEST

Take the test 'Ideal parents – Les parents idéaux' at www.brightredbooks.net/N5French

 VIDEO LINK

Watch 'Family and children' at www.brightredbooks.net/N5French

FRIENDSHIP – L'AMITIÉ

Although we have touched on friendship already and some of the phrases we have learned can be used to describe your friendships, we are now going to focus on how you spend time with your friends and peer pressure.

ACTIVITY: SPENDING TIME WITH YOUR FAMILY/ FRIENDS – PASSER DU TEMPS AVEC SA FAMILLE/SES AMIS

Listen to the following conversation between two people discussing their friends. Fill in the gaps using the words in the box below. Before listening to the audio track, read through the text and predict what you might hear.

A: J'ai de la chance car ma _____ amie et moi, nous avons les mêmes _____.
On s'amuse bien à faire les _____ le samedi après-midi et le samedi soir, on _____ bien quand nous allons au cinéma. On adore regarder les films _____.
Et toi, Jean-Claude, est-ce tu passes beaucoup de temps avec tes amis?

B: Ah oui. On passe des heures ensemble à jouer au foot car on fait _____ du même club de foot. Ce que _____ le plus c'est participer aux matchs de foot le _____ matin avec mes amis.

A: Est-ce que tu as un meilleur ami?

B: Oui, il s'appelle Philippe et il est _____ et vraiment sympa. On _____ aux mêmes sports, donc on regarde les sports à la _____. Je peux compter sur lui et si j'ai un problème, il _____ et il me donne de bons _____.

A: Selon moi, le plus important c'est qu'on est sur la même _____ _____. J'aime bien discuter de tout avec ma meilleure amie et je peux lui faire _____.

drôle	magasins	m'aide	rigole	j'aime	meilleure	s'intéresse	conseils
samedi	confiance	comiques	intérêts	télé	partie	longueur d'onde	

ACTIVITY: RELATIONSHIPS WITH FRIENDS – LES RAPPORTS AVEC SES AMIS

Read the following phrases and decide if the phrases are describing a good friend or a bad friend. Listen to the audio track to help with pronunciation. You might want to practise translating the phrases into English.

1. Il/elle me comprend.
2. Il/elle ne me critique pas.
3. Il/elle m'encourage rarement.
4. Il/elle ne me soutient jamais.
5. Il/elle m'énerve.
6. Il/elle n'est pas embêtant(e).
7. Il/elle n'est jamais jaloux(-se).
8. Il/elle m'ennuie.
9. Il/elle a le sens de l'humour.
10. Il/elle se plaint tout le temps.
11. Il/elle n'est pas égoïste.
12. Il/elle me respecte.
13. Il/elle ne m'écoute jamais.
14. Je peux me confier à lui/elle.
15. Il/elle m'ignore à l'école.
16. Il/elle est toujours là quand j'ai besoin de quelqu'un.
17. Il/elle se dispute pour n'importe quoi.

ACTIVITY: TRANSLATING THE CONDITIONAL TENSE

Put the phrases above into the conditional tense to describe what a good friend *would* do, then translate them into English. You might need to turn some phrases into negative sentences (refer back to the notes on negatives on page 8).

Here are a few to start you off:

1. Un bon ami me comprend**rait**.

2. Un bon ami **ne me** critique**rait pas**.

3. Il/elle m'encourage**rait**.

Write a paragraph about your friends. You might want to include what makes a good friend and how you spend time with your friends. You may wish to use this as part of your Performance.

PEER PRESSURE – L'INFLUENCE DES PAIRS

When we are talking about friendship, peer pressure often arises as a topic for discussion. Read the following phrases and decide if the person in each sentence is influenced by his/her peers or not.

- J'aime me sentir à l'aise avec mes amis donc je fais comme mes amis.
- Je fais ce que je veux sans m'inquiéter des avis des autres jeunes.
- Je me sens le mieux quand je suis au sein d'un groupe d'amis.
- J'ai peur des opinions et du jugement des autres.
- J'ai envie d'être original et différent de mes amis.
- Je ne veux pas me sentir isolé(e) ou seul(e).
- J'ai l'habitude de m'habiller comme mes amis.
- J'ai de la chance car je ne fais pas attention à ce que mes amis pensent.
- Ce que j'aime le plus, c'est qu'on porte ce qu'on veut.
- J'ai du mal à montrer ma personnalité à mes amis.

- J'ai envie de m'intégrer à une bande donc je dois être comme les autres.
- J'ai besoin d'acheter les vêtements de marques.
- J'ai l'occasion de sortir avec mes amis tous les week-ends et je ne voudrais pas être exclu(e).
- J'ai de la chance car mes amis ne me jugent jamais.
- Je fume comme tous mes amis afin d'avoir l'air cool.
- Je dois toujours suivre mes amis, ce qui m'énerve de temps en temps.
- J'ai de la chance car je peux m'identifier à mes amis et on n'est pas obligé d'avoir les mêmes goûts.
- Je trouve ça difficile de résister à l'influence des pairs car je ne veux pas être différent(e).

ONLINE TEST

Take the test 'Friendship – L'amitié' at www.brightredbooks.net/N5French

ONLINE

Check out the link 'Conditional tense' at www.brightredbooks.net/N5French

DON'T FORGET

Ce que and *ce qui* are called **relative pronouns**. You will notice *ce qui* and *ce que* in these phrases. Can you work out what they mean?

THINGS TO DO AND THINK ABOUT

From the sentences about peer pressure, can you pick out any **avoir phrases**? Here is a list of some useful avoir phrases. Do you know what they mean?

- Avoir besoin de
- Avoir envie de
- Avoir peur de
- Avoir l'occasion de

- Avoir de la chance de
- Avoir du mal à
- Avoir l'air
- Avoir soif

- Avoir faim
- Avoir chaud
- Avoir froid

Can you make up a sentence using each of these avoir phrases?

PEOPLE WHO INFLUENCE ME – LES GENS QUI M'INFLUENCENT

PHRASES THAT EXPRESS WHO INFLUENCES YOU AND WHY

If you are asked who influences you, you might think of a member of your family. Here are some phrases to express who influences you and why.

- Ma famille m'inspire – My family inspires me
- Ma famille m'influence, chacun à leur façon – My family influence me, each in their own way
- Mon frère joue un rôle très important dans ma vie – My brother plays a very important role in my life
- Je trouve que ma mère m'influence beaucoup – I find that my mum influences me a lot
- La personne qui m'influence le plus, c'est mon père – The person who influences me the most is my dad
- Mes parents peuvent influencer mes choix– My parents can influence my choices
- Une personne qui m'influence dans ma vie est mon grand-père – One person who influences me in life is my grandfather
- Mon (ma) meilleur(e) ami(e) influence mes décisions – My best friend influences my decisions

Here are some reasons why:

- … car il/elle est sage – because he/she is wise
- … car je passe la plupart de mon temps libre avec lui/elle – because I spend most of my free time with him/her
- … car je le/la respecte – because I respect him/her
- … car il/elle me donne de bons conseils– because he/she gives me good advice
- … car il/elle a toujours raison – because he/she is always right

DON'T FORGET

Remember to adapt the phrases and learn them so you can choose to use them in your Performance.

ONLINE TEST

Take the test 'People who influence me – Les gens qui m'influencent' at www.brightredbooks.net/N5French

 ACTIVITY: PEER PRESSURE AND INFLUENCE -

Write a paragraph about whether or not you feel peer pressure and about the people who influence you. Again, this could be used as part of your Performance.

RELATIONSHIPS WITH FAMILY AND FRIENDS: RECAP

By the end of this section, you should have written various paragraphs on the following topics:

Who is in your family: personal information (name, age, description)

What they are like: physical description, personal qualities (positive and negative)

Your relationship with them: why you get on well, what you do together

Any conflicts there might be: the reasons for arguments

Ideal relationships: ideal parents, ideal brothers and sisters, ideal friendships

Influences: peer pressure, other people who influence you

You should also feel confident about the following grammar points:

- present tense of regular and irregular verbs
- adjective agreements
- negatives
- conditional tense
- avoir phrases.

Test yourself: Vocabulary

Can you recall and write down:

- three positive adjectives?
- three negative adjectives?
- three positive phrases about your relationship with your family?
- three negative phrases about your relationship with your family?
- three phrases about ideal parents?
- three phrases about what you do with your friends/family?
- three phrases about peer pressure?

Test yourself: Knowledge about language

Can you recall:

- the rule about adjective agreements?
- six negatives?
- how to form the present tense?
- how to form the conditional tense?
- three avoir phrases?
- three adverbs of frequency?
- what *ce qui* and *ce que* mean?

THINGS TO DO AND THINK ABOUT

You have learned a lot in this section and used your listening, reading, dictionary and writing skills, as well as learning vocabulary and grammar rules. Following the 'Test yourself' tasks, is there any area that you are not sure of? If so, look over this section again and revise the vocabulary or grammar that is causing you difficulty.

LEISURE – LES LOISIRS 1

You will know quite a lot of vocabulary already about *les loisirs*, like different types of sports and hobbies. When thinking about your hobbies, you could mention the following:

Quand?

Avec qui?

Mon passe-temps préféré, c'est ...

Où?

Les opinions?

Pourquoi?

VIDEO LINK

Check out the clip 'Leisure activities in the country' at www.brightredbooks.net/N5French

VIDEO LINK

Have a look at the clip 'Les loisirs – la musique' at www.brightredbooks.net/N5French

REVISION – LA RÉVISION

It is useful to be able to say how often you do your hobbies, when, with whom, why and where, which you could include in a piece of writing or as part of your Performance.

Here are a few phrases to start you off. Can you work out what they mean?

Mon passe-temps préféré, c'est ...

- jouer au tennis
- faire de la natation
- la lecture

- aller au cinéma
- faire du shopping
- regarder la télé

- faire de l'équitation
- faire les magasins.

VIDEO LINK

Watch the clip 'Avec la famille' to hear children talking about what they do with their family, at www.brightredbooks.net/N5French

Avec qui?

- Avec mes amis/mes copains
- Avec mon père/ma mère
- Je suis membre d'un club

- Je fais partie d'une équipe
- Tout(e) seul(e)

Quand?

- Le samedi matin
- Le mardi après les cours
- Le mercredi soir
- Le dimanche après-midi

- Une fois par semaine
- Trois fois par mois
- Souvent
- Quelquefois

- De temps en temps
- Rarement

contd

Où?

- Au parc
- Au terrain de foot/golf
- Au centre-ville
- Chez moi
- Au centre sportif
- Dans le jardin

Les opinions?

- J'adore ...
- J'aime ...
- Je me passionne
- Je m'intéresse

Pourquoi?

- C'est amusant
- C'est passionnant
- C'est divertissant
- C'est relaxant
- Je peux rencontrer de nouvelles personnes
- Ça m'aide à me détendre
- C'est un bon moyen de s'échapper du stress de la vie scolaire
- C'est bon pour la santé
- Ça me tient en bonne forme

DON'T FORGET

Look at the section on healthy living to find more reasons for why you do your hobbies.

HOBBIES – LES PASSE-TEMPS

The following list is a reminder of some of the more difficult vocabulary to do with hobbies. Can you remember what the following words/phrases mean? If not, look up any unfamiliar vocabulary in the dictionary.

- Faire du cheval
- Faire du shopping
- Faire du vélo
- Faire du VTT
- Faire de l'escalade
- Faire de la voile
- Faire de la planche à voile
- Faire de la plongée
- Faire de la randonnée
- Faire des sports aquatiques
- Faire les courses/les magasins
- Faire une promenade
- Faire une balade à vélo/à bateau
- Nager
- Lire des romans
- Sortir avec mes amis
- Passer du temps avec mes amis
- Aller à une fête/en boite/à une soirée
- Aller au cinéma/au théâtre
- Aller à la piscine
- Regarder la télé/les films
- Ecouter de la musique sur mon iPod
- Passer des heures sur Internet/sur Facebook
- Bavarder avec mes amis sur mon portable
- Rendre visite à quelqu'un

DON'T FORGET

Some of these phrases are translated into English with a different verb, for example *faire une promenade* means 'to go for a walk'.

THINGS TO DO AND THINK ABOUT

Don't forget to revise "les verbes irréguliers"!

To describe what you do during your free time, you need to know verbs in the present tense. Refer to page 7 to revise how to form the present tense and 'er', 'ir' and 're' verb endings.

ONLINE TEST

Why not try the 'Irregular verbs' online test to revise these, including aller and faire, at www.brightredbooks.net/N5French.

LEISURE – LES LOISIRS 2

TO DO SPORT – FAIRE DU SPORT

To say which sports and hobbies you do, you need to know the verb faire.

If the sport or hobby:

- is masculine, then faire is followed by *du*, for example *le judo – faire du judo*
- is feminine, then faire is followed by *de la*, for example *la natation – faire de la natation*
- begins with a vowel or a silent 'h', faire is followed by *de l'*, for example *l'athlétisme – faire de l'athlétisme*
- is plural, then faire is followed by *des*, for example *les sports aquatiques – faire des sports aquatiques.*

VIDEO LINK

Watch the clip 'Sport and leisure activities in Marseille' at www.brightredbooks.net/N5French

⚙ ACTIVITY: TO DO SPORT – FAIRE DU SPORT

Translate the following sentences into French using the correct part of faire and *du, de la, de l'* or *des*.

1. I go cycling.
2. He goes mountain biking.
3. She goes swimming.
4. We go hiking.
5. They (masculine) go horse-riding.
6. I go windsurfing.
7. You (formal) go sailing.
8. They (feminine) do water sports.

VIDEO LINK

Check out the clip 'Le sport' to hear about different sports which are practiced in Sénégal at www.brightredbooks.net/N5French

TO GO TO THE TOWN CENTRE – ALLER AU CENTRE-VILLE

Aller is another very important irregular verb that you need to know. There are different ways of saying 'to the' in French, depending on whether the place:

- is masculine, for example *le parc –Je vais au parc*
- is feminine, for example *la piscine – Je vais à la piscine*
- begins with a vowel or silent h, for example *l'école' – Je vais à l'école*
- is plural, for example *les magasins – Je vais aux magasins.*

ACTIVITY: TO GO TO THE ... – ALLER AU/À LA/À L'/AUX ...

Translate the following sentences into French using the correct part of aller and *au, à la, à l'* or *aux*.

1. I am going to the cinema.

2. He is going to the sports centre.

3. She is going to the beach.

4. We are going to the shops.

5. They (masculine) are going to the theatre.

6. I am going to the shopping centre.

7. You (formal) are going to the restaurant.

8. They (feminine) are going to the hotel.

 ACTIVITY: OPINIONS – LES OPINIONS

It is a good idea to revise opinion phrases in more detail at this stage. Read and listen to the following passage and pick out all the opinion phrases. You may wish to try to include them in your writing and Performance.

Jacques

Je crois que je suis très sportif. J'adore passer mon temps libre à faire du sport. Mon sport préféré, c'est le basket. Ce que j'aime le plus, c'est jouer au basket avec mes amis car on s'amuse bien à jouer en équipe. Je pense que ma sœur n'aime pas le basket. Elle préfère nager car elle dit que c'est bon pour la santé. Elle s'entraîne trois fois par semaine et elle adore ça. En ce qui me concerne, j'ai horreur de la natation car ça me fatigue et je trouve ça ennuyeux. Mon père s'intéresse au sport aussi et on passe des heures à regarder le sport à la télé. Il croit que ça aide à se détendre après avoir passé la journée au travail. Ma mère déteste le sport à la télé. Elle préfère regarder des films romantiques, ce que je trouve barbant. En effet, elle préférerait passer des heures à lire un bon roman au lieu de regarder la télé. Elle pense que c'est un bon moyen d'échapper à la vie de tous les jours.

As well as picking out the key opinion phrases, can you note down what each person enjoys doing in their free time and why?

 THINGS TO DO AND THINK ABOUT

You should revise other sports and hobbies, opinions and adverbs of time in French at this stage to refresh your memory. Write a paragraph on how you spend your free time and try to include some of the fancier phrases. Include when you do these hobbies, how often, where and with whom. You might also want to refer to the section on using technology and the internet in your free time (refer to pages 38–9). This paragraph can be used as a piece of writing and also as part of your Performance.

 VIDEO LINK

For a great clip about what leisure activities people get up to at the weekend, watch the clip 'Les loisirs – le weekend' at www. brightredbooks.net/N5French

 ONLINE TEST

Try the 'Leisure – Les loisirs' test online at www. brightredbooks.net/N5French

 DON'T FORGET

If you are unsure about whether a verb is regular or irregular, check the verb section in your bilingual dictionary. This section will also give you examples of the verb formed in different tenses.

HEALTHY LIFESTYLE – LA VIE SAINE 1

In this section you will learn to talk about what you do to stay healthy. We will divide it into what physical exercise we do and what we eat and drink to keep healthy.

USEFUL VOCABULARY

Here is some useful vocabulary that will help you to describe how to stay healthy. Spend a few minutes looking at this vocabulary and then cover up the English meanings. How many of these words you can remember? Revise the ones that you are having difficulty with and then cover the English again to see if you can remember them all. Leave it for a while and then come back to this vocabulary. How many can you remember now?

il faut + infinitive	it is necessary to/you must
il ne faut pas + infinitive	it is not necessary to/you must not
on doit + infinitive	we must
on ne doit pas + infinitive	we must not
boire de l'eau	to drink water
contrôler le stress	to control stress
dormir	to sleep
être en bonne santé	to be in good health
faire de l'exercice	to do exercise
faire attention à sa santé	to take care of your health
faire du sport	to do sport
manger cinq portions de fruits ou légumes par jour	to eat five portions of fruit and vegetables per day
manger de la nourriture fraîche	to eat fresh food
mener une vie active	to lead an active life
rester en bonne forme	to stay fit
suivre un régime sain	to follow a healthy diet
suivre un régime équilibé	to follow a balanced diet
trouver l'équilibre entre le travail et les loisirs	to find the balance between work and leisure
boire des boissons gazeuses	to drink fizzy drinks
éviter les sucreries	to avoid sweet things
éviter les matières grasses	to avoid fatty foods
prendre du poids/grossir	to put on weight

DON'T FORGET

Il faut means 'it is necessary to' or 'you must' and can be used in lots of different contexts. It is followed by the infinitive.

DON'T FORGET

On doit is part of the verb *devoir*. Devoir belongs to an important group of irregular verbs called modal verbs.

MODAL VERBS

A **modal verb** is a verb associated with possibility or necessity, such as can, could, may, might, must, shall, should, will and would. In French, the modal verbs are:

vouloir – to want to
Je veux jouer au foot – I want to play football
Je voudrais jouer au foot – I would like to play football

devoir – to have to/must
Je dois manger sainement – I have to/must eat healthily
On devrait manger sain – We should eat healthily

pouvoir – to be able to/can
Je peux faire du sport – I am able to/can do sport
On pourrait manger plus de légumes – We could eat more vegetables

ONLINE

Take the 'Using modal verbs' test online at www.brightredbooks.net/N5French

VIDEO LINK

Watch the clip 'Healthy living and fitness' at www.brightredbooks.net/N5French

contd

savoir – to know how to
Je sais manger sainement – I know how to eat healthily
On sait mener une vie active – We know how to lead an active life

⚙ ACTIVITY: HEALTHY LIVING

Read the following texts and answer the questions in English. Here are some tips for how to approach a reading comprehension for the Course and Unit reading assessments.

- You might want to read the questions first before skimming over the passage in French. This will give you an idea of what the text is about before you even begin to read the French.
- You might want to think about the type of vocabulary you are looking for in the text, for example if the question asks you when something happens, you will need to think about time phrases.
- Looking at the number of marks given for each answer will indicate how much information you need to look for.
- When you skim the text, find the parts of the passage that answer the questions by spotting key words.
- Then take each question at a time and read the text more closely, looking up any unfamiliar vocabulary in the dictionary.

Pierre

En ce qui concerne la santé, il est important de manger équilibré pour satisfaire nos besoins nutritionnels. Il faut varier l'alimentation et éviter les matières grasses et sucrées comme les pizzas, les frites, les chips et le chocolat car si on mange des aliments trop gras et trop sucrés, on peut devenir obèse. L'obésité peut mener à des maladies comme le diabète ou les maladies du cœur. Si on mange de la viande et du poisson, on a une source de protéines et de fer. Comme source de fibre, de vitamines et de minéraux, il faut manger des fruits et des légumes. En plus, les produits laitiers, comme le lait et le fromage, apportent du calcium, ce qui est important pour le corps. Je dirais que l'eau est essentielle pour l'hydratation et il faut boire au moins deux litres d'eau par jour. Par contre, il faut éviter de boire trop de caféine et d'alcool afin de rester en bonne santé. Finalement, je pense qu'il faut prendre l'habitude de manger de tout, en quantité raisonnable.

1. Why does Pierre think eating a balanced diet is important? (1)
2. What does he think you should avoid and why? (2)
3. What can obesity lead to? (2)
4. What do meat and fish provide us with? (2)
5. What should we eat in order to have fibre, vitamins and minerals? (2)
6. Which two examples of dairy products does Pierre mention? (2)
7. What does Pierre say about water? (2)
8. What does he think you should avoid drinking? (2)

Thérèse

A l'égard de la santé, je sais qu'il est nécessaire de manger une alimentation équilibrée et saine. Pour ma part, j'aime bien manger des matières grasses et des sucreries comme le chocolat et les bonbons. En plus j'adore boire des boissons gazeuses même si je sais qu'elles contiennent beaucoup de sucre. C'est vrai que je grignotte beaucoup pour me consoler car cette année il y a beaucoup de pression à l'école. Donc je prends du poids et je me sens déprimée. Pour perdre du poids, j'ai commencé à sauter les repas mais je sais que ce n'est pas une bonne idée. Je dors mal et pendant les cours au lycée, je ne peux pas me concentrer à cause de cette perte de sommeil et de cette fatigue. Je mange au McDo avec mes amis deux fois par semaine et, à mon avis, c'est génial car le service est rapide et ce n'est pas cher. Ma mère dit que le fast-food n'est pas bon pour la santé. Elle a horreur des produits gras comme les hamburgers et les frites car ils contiennent trop de calories.

1. What does Thérèse like to eat? (2)
2. What does she like to drink? (1)
3. Why does Thérèse eat so many snacks? (2)
4. What has caused Thérèse to feel depressed? (1)
5. What has she started doing to lose weight? (1)
6. Thérèse finds it difficult to sleep. What problem is this causing? (1)
7. Why does Thérèse like McDonalds? (2)
8. Give two reasons why Thérèse's mum does not approve of fast-food restaurants. (2)

THINGS TO DO AND THINK ABOUT

If there are any useful phrases about what to eat and drink to stay healthy and what to avoid, take a note of these and learn them so you may wish to use them in your Performance.

HEALTHY LIFESTYLE – LA VIE SAINE 2

Now we will look at other ways of staying healthy and focus on doing physical exercise and keeping fit.

⚙ ACTIVITY: KEEPING FIT

Listen to three people talking about what they do to keep fit. Fill in the blanks using the vocabulary in the boxes below each section. Read through the text first and try to predict what you might hear. Use the dictionary to look up any unfamiliar vocabulary.

Alain

Pour être en forme, il faut faire régulièrement de _____ _____ et suivre un régime _____ sain. J'aime bien le tennis et j'y joue _____ cinq ans. Je suis très _____ et je m'amuse bien quand je joue au tennis avec mes amis. Quand j'étais plus jeune, j'ai joué au golf avec mon père. En été, j'ai passe des heures au _____. Je trouve que maintenant j'ai trop de devoirs à faire donc je n'ai pas assez du temps pour _____ au golf et au tennis. J'ai dû choisir entre les deux sports et comme aucun de mes amis ne joue au golf, j'ai décidé de _____ à jouer au tennis. Je ne passe pas beaucoup de temps devant _____, comme la télé ou l'ordinateur parce que je me rends compte que si on veut _____ la forme, on doit faire de l'exercice physique.

| l'exercice physique | jouer | continuer | alimentaire | depuis | les écrans | garder |
| compétitif | terrain de golf | aérobic |

Brigitte

Je dois admettre que je ne suis pas très _____. Je n'aime pas vraiment le sport et je préfère lire un bon livre ou regarder un film au ciné puisque ça ___ _____. Je n'ai pas la motivation pour aller au _____ ou pour faire du sport. Au lycée, je joue au _____ pendant les cours d'EPS. C'est rigolo mais très fatigant. Pour rester en bonne santé, je vais au lycée __ _____ au lieu de prendre le bus. En plus, je monte _____ à pied au lieu de prendre l' _____. Je sais qu'un manque d'activité physique peut être à l'origine des _____. Quand je serai plus grande, je n'ai pas envie de devenir _____. Par conséquent, après avoir quitté le lycée, j'ai _____ de faire plus d'exercice physique.

| gymnase | active | me détend | obèse | ascenseur | basket | maladies | à pied |
| l'escalier | l'intention |

Antoine

Ce que j'aime le plus, c'est la _____. Je suis membre d'un club et je vais à _____ quatre fois par semaine. La semaine dernière j'ai participé à un _____ de natation. Je n'ai pas gagné mais _____ amusant car j'ai des amis qui font partie du même club de natation. L'entraînement commence à six heures le matin donc avant d'aller au lycée je dois __ _____ tôt et aller à la _____. Il est important de __ _____ assez tôt aussi, toujours avant 22 heures. Je trouve que la natation m'aide à contrôler le stress et à mon avis, il faut traver _____ entre le travail au lycée et les loisirs. J'ai de la chance car je ne suis pas souvent _____ grâce à ma vie active et saine.

| malade | concours | natation | piscine | me lever | l'entraînement | c'était |
| me coucher | l'équilibre |

KNOWLEDGE ABOUT LANGUAGE

In the listening texts, you heard phrases in the **perfect tense** (*j'ai joué*), the **simple future** tense (*je serai*) and the **imperfect tense** (*c'était*). To revise the perfect and imperfect tenses, see pages 43 and 67–9.

The simple future – Le futur simple

The simple future tense is used to describe an action that *will* happen in the future. It is similar to the conditional tense in how it is formed:

1. First write down the subject (person who is doing the verb): *Je.*
2. Then write down the infinitive: *Je jouer.*
3. Now add the simple future endings to the infinitive: *Je jouerai* – I will play (although take off the 'e' at the end of 're' verbs before adding the endings, e.g. *Je prendrai* – I will take).

The simple future endings are:

je	-ai	nous	-ons
tu	-as	vous	-ez
il/elle/on	-a	ils/elles	-ont

 ACTIVITY: THE SIMPLE FUTURE – LE FUTUR SIMPLE

Now translate the following sentences using the simple future tense:

1. I will spend less time watching TV.
2. I will eat healthily.
3. I will play football with my friends.
4. We will drink two litres of water per day.
5. We will avoid fatty foods.

IRREGULAR FUTURE STEMS

The key irregular future stems that you need to know include:

- avoir – j'aurai (I will have)
- être – je serai (I will be)
- faire – je ferai (I will do/make)
- aller – j'irai (I will go)
- vouloir – je voudrai (I will like)
- pouvoir – je pourrai (I will be able to/could)
- devoir – je devrai (I will have to/should).

 ACTIVITY: IRREGULAR VERBS IN THE SIMPLE FUTURE TENSE – LES IRRÉGULIERS AU FUTUR SIMPLE

Translate the following sentences into French using the irregular conditional stems:

1. I will go to the gym.
2. I will do more sport.
3. I will have to do more physical exercise.
4. We will be able to stay fit.
5. We will be more active.

 # THINGS TO DO AND THINK ABOUT

Can you write down ten sentences to do with staying healthy? Try to include phrases about both eating habits and an active lifestyle (including what to avoid in order to stay fit and healthy).

You might also want to include phrases in different tenses. Try to mention the following:

- what you do to keep healthy at the moment (present tense)
- what you used to do (imperfect tense)
- what you will do in future (future tense)
- what you would do if you had more time (conditional tense).

 DON'T FORGET

Se lever and *se coucher* are **reflexive verbs**.

 ONLINE TEST

Take the 'La vie saine' test online at www.brightredbooks.net/N5French

 VIDEO LINK

Watch the clip 'Le sport' at www.brightredbooks.net/N5French

LIFESTYLE-RELATED ILLNESSES – LES MALADIES

We have looked at ways of staying healthy. Now we are going to learn to talk about unhealthy lifestyles. In this section we will look at why people choose to smoke, drink alcohol or take drugs and what the consequences are.

BRAINSTORMING VOCABULARY

There are many illnesses that are caused by unhealthy lifestyles. Can you think of any lifestyle choices that could cause different illnesses? Here are some words to help you get started:

Boire de l'alcool
Fumer
Se droguer
Le manque d'exercice
Les maladies
Le cancer
L'obésité
Une maladie cardiovasculaire

GENERAL VOCABULARY

Here is some general vocabulary that is useful to know. Cover the English meanings and 'traffic light' the vocabulary you already know. Then focus on the vocabulary you don't know and learn it.

le tabagisme	smoking
fumer des cigarettes	to smoke cigarettes
consommer l'alcool	to consume alcohol
essayer l'alcool	to try alcohol
être nuisible à la santé	to be harmful to your health
prendre de la drogue	to take drugs
se droguer	to take drugs
la dépendance	addiction
la toxicomanie	drug addiction

DON'T FORGET ➕

To work out who doesn't smoke or drink alcohol, you need to look out for negative words. Look back to page 9 to revise the different negatives in French.

DON'T FORGET ➕

You will notice how *j'ai peur* and *je n'ai pas envie* are used in some sentences. Look back to page 19 to revise avoir phrases.

⚙ **ACTIVITY:** SMOKING AND ALCOHOL – LE TABAC ET L'ALCOOL

You might want to think about why people choose to make their lifestyle choices. Read and listen to the phrases below. First, decide if the person talking smokes or drinks alcohol or doesn't smoke or drink alcohol. Then try to work out why, looking up any words you don't know in the dictionary. After translating the phrases into English, choose which ones apply to you and memorise them as these can be used in your Performance.

Listening to the phrases online will help you with the pronunciation.

- Je ne bois pas d'alcool car ce n'est pas bon pour la santé.
- Je bois de l'alcool car ça me donne confiance en moi.
- Je ne fume plus car le tabagisme coûte trop cher.
- Je bois de l'alcool car j'ai envie d'échapper aux soucis de tous les jours.
- Je ne fume jamais car c'est nuisible pour la santé.

contd

- Je ne bois jamais d'alcool car ça a un effet négatif sur le comportement.
- Je bois de l'alcool car je ne veux pas être différent(e) de mes amis.
- Je ne bois pas d'alcool car mes parents ne me feraient plus confiance.
- Je fume car ça m'aide à me relaxer.
- Je bois de l'alcool car tous mes amis boivent de l'alcool.
- Je fume car c'est une habitude et c'est mon choix.
- Je bois de l'alcool car ça m'aide à me sentir plus à l'aise.
- Je ne fume pas car il y a un risque de dépendance.
- Je ne bois pas d'alcool car mes parents seraient en colère contre moi.
- Je fume car je pense qu'on a l'air cool.
- Même si je suis entouré(e) de personnes qui fument, je n'ai pas envie de fumer car c'est dangereux pour la santé.
- Tous mes problèmes disparaissent quand je bois de l'alcool.
- Je ne fume jamais car j'ai peur que je ne pourrais pas m'arrêter.
- Je fume car ça me détend quand je suis stressé(e).
- Je ne bois pas d'alcool car je n'aime pas le goût et je ne fume pas car ça sent mauvais.

For an extra activity on lifestyle-related illnesses, head to the BrightRED Digital Zone.

 ACTIVITY: WHY DO PEOPLE SMOKE OR DRINK ALCOHOL? – POURQUOI EST-CE QU'ON FUME OU BOIT DE L'ALCOOL?

Listen to the following three people talk about their lifestyles. Fill in the blanks using the words below.

Frédéric

J'ai envie d'être comme mes _____ donc je fume. Tous mes amis _____ des cigarettes alors c'est vrai que je suis toujours entouré de personnes qui fument. Je pense que nous avons _____ cool. C'est mon choix et je suis _____ quand je fume. En effet, je dirais que fumer, ça _____ à me détendre. Je sais qu'il y a des _____ comme le cancer mais je ne veux pas m'arrêter.

> amis   heureux   fument   aide   l'air   risques

Sandrine

Je bois de _____ depuis deux ans. Mes parents me laissent boire _____ de vin de temps en temps. Quand je sors avec mes amis, je bois de l'alcool car ça me donne _____ en moi. Il est vrai que la plupart de mes amis boivent de l'alcool _____ et il y en a qui boivent trop. Ce que je n'aime pas, c'est quand ils sont _____ car l'alcool a un effet très négatif sur le _____, ce qui peut être vraiment gênant.

> confiance   ivres   comportement   l'alcool   un verre   régulièrement

Jean-Luc

Il y a trois semaines, je suis sorti avec mes copains le vendredi soir. Un de mes amis m'a _____ du cannabis mais j'ai refusé d'en prendre. Parfois je bois de l'alcool et je fume mais je n'ai pas envie de prendre de la _____. Je la trouve dangereuse car, en _____, on peut devenir _____. Je sais que si on se drogue, on peut avoir une sensation de peur, de fatigue et une perte du sommeil. Le plus grave c'est que si on prend une _____ de drogue, on peut mourir. En plus, si mes parents savaient que j'avais essayé le cannabis, ils seraient en _____ et ils ne me laisseraient plus de liberté.

> surdose   drogue   colère   essayant   dépendant   offert

 VIDEO LINK

Check out 'Le fast food' at www.brightredbooks.net/ N5French

 ONLINE TEST

Take the test 'Les maladies' at www.brightredbooks.net/ N5French

DON'T FORGET

Depuis means 'since' or for' and when used with a present tense verb it means you *have been doing* that verb for a certain length of time, for example *Je joue au foot depuis deux ans* means 'I have been playing football for two years'. *Il y a* usually means 'there is' or 'there are' but when it is followed by a time phrase, it means 'ago', for example *il y a deux semaines* means 'two weeks ago'.

 DON'T FORGET

The small word *en* is very useful, it can mean 'of it' or 'of them', depending on the context, e.g. *il y en a* means 'there are some of them'.

 THINGS TO DO AND THINK ABOUT

Are there any phrases from these activities that you could use or that you could adapt? Jot down the phrases that apply to you and learn them as you may wish to use them for your Performance.

TELEVISION – LA TÉLÉ

In this section, you will learn to describe what you watch on TV.

DON'T FORGET

Be careful! Some French words might look like English words, but they actually mean something different, such as *les informations* which means 'news' in English. These words are known as *faux amis* or 'false friends'. To be on the safe side, look up any words which are unfamiliar to you in the dictionary.

USEFUL VOCABULARY

Here is some useful vocabulary to revise what we watch on TV. Match the French vocabulary to the correct image. Try to work out what the French vocabulary means by making links to English vocabulary, for example *une comédie* is 'a comedy' in English.

Les informations/les actualités
Les documentaires (sur la nature/l'histoire)
Les émissions de sport/de musique
Les dessins-animés
Les feuilletons
Un jeu télévisé
La publicité
La météo
Un western

Une comédie
Un film d'aventure
Un film de guerre
Un film de science-fiction
Un film policier
Un film d'espionnage
Un drame psychologique
Un film d'horreur
Un film romantique

contd

THINGS TO DO AND THINK ABOUT

Want to see how you did? Get the answers at the Bright Red Digital Zone online at
www.brightredbooks.net/N5French

 ONLINE TEST

Try the 'False friends'
test online at www.
brightredbooks.net/N5French

WATCHING TV – REGARDER LA TÉLÉ

As well as saying what you watch on TV, it would be good to be able to say how long you spend watching TV and what you enjoy watching, with reasons for your opinions.

⚙ ACTIVITY: OPINIONS OF DIFFERENT PROGRAMMES – LES OPINIONS DES ÉMISSIONS DIFFÉRENTES

Listen to the following text and fill in the blanks using the words below. Read the text first and try to predict what you might hear, using the context as a basis for your prediction. Look up any new words in the dictionary before you start.

Sandra

Je passe environ deux heures par jour devant le petit _____. J'aime surtout regarder les _____ et les comédies. Je les trouve _____ et pour moi, c'est un bon moyen de ___ _____ car je ne dois pas trop me concentrer.

écran   me détendre   feuilletons   divertissants

Anna

Je ne passe pas beaucoup de temps à regarder la télé car c'est une _____ de temps. Il y a trop de jeunes qui regardent la télé _____ _____ et ce n'est pas bon pour la santé. Si je regarde la télé, je préfère regarder les _____ et les émissions qui m'instruisent et qui _____.

m'informent   perte   documentaires   sans arrêt

Christophe

Normalement, je n'ai pas assez de temps pour regarder la télé ___ _____ car j'ai trop de devoirs. Le vendredi soir, j'adore regarder les films _____ et les films d'horreur avec mes amis car je les trouve _____. Le samedi soir, ma famille et moi aimons regarder les ____ _____. Je pense qu'ils sont rigolos et quelquefois, il y a des questions difficiles, alors on peut apprendre des choses.

en semaine   passionnants   jeux télévisés   policiers

Simon

Je regarde les informations et __ _____ à la télé donc je ne passe qu'une heure par jour devant le petit écran. Je crois que la télé est un bon moyen de _____ et de découvrir ce qui se passe dans le _____ entier. Ce qui est bien, c'est qu'on peut voir les images en direct, donc c'est plus _____ que la radio.

communiquer   monde   frappant   la météo

contd

Céline

Je passe la plupart de mon temps libre à regarder la télé. Ma mère dit que je suis
_____ à la télé-réalité. Mon émission préférée s'appelle 'Top Chef' et je ne _____
jamais un épisode. Ma mère pense que c'est une émission superficielle et _____.
Elle m'encourage à faire d'autres choses plus actives car elle a peur que la télé ne me
rende _____.

bête   rate   accro   paresseuse

PRECEDING DIRECT OBJECTS

You will notice *je le trouve, je la trouve* and *je les trouve* appear in some of the reading and listening texts. In these phrases *le, la* and *les* are known as **preceding direct objects**. Can you guess what they mean from the contexts?

Look at the examples and their translations and work out the grammar rule:

a. J'adore le sport. Je le regarde à la télé tous les jours.
   I love sport. I watch it on TV every day.

b. J'adore ma jupe. Je la porte souvent.
   I love my skirt. I often wear it.

c. Je n'aime pas mes voisins, je les déteste!
   I don't like my neighbours, I hate them!

Le and *la* are translated as 'it' and *les* is translated as 'them'. The preceding direct object must agree with the noun it refers to in terms of gender and number.

DON'T FORGET

Ne ... jamais is a negative phrase. Refer to pages 8–9 to revise negatives. Negatives usually sandwich the verb. When using a negative phrase with a preceding direct object, the negatives sandwich both the preceding direct object and the verb, for example *je ne le regarde jamais* – I never watch it.

VIDEO LINK

Check out the clip 'My favourite films and directors' at www.brightredbooks.net/N5French

ONLINE TEST

Try the 'Watching TV – Regarder la télé' test online at www.brightredbooks.net/N5French

ACTIVITY:

Now try to translate the following sentences using the correct preceding direct object.

1. I like westerns. I watch them often.

2. I love comedies. I watch them at weekends.

3. I don't like documentaries. I watch them rarely.

4. I hate football. I watch it sometimes.

5. I like the weather. I watch it every day.

6. I don't like crime films. I never watch them.

THINGS TO DO AND THINK ABOUT

Now write a paragraph about how much time you spend watching TV, what you watch on TV and why. Refer back to the section on opinion phrases on page 25 and try to include them. You may wish to use this as part of your Performance if you talk about what you do during your free time.

REALITY TV – LA TÉLÉ-RÉALITÉ

Reality TV shows have become very popular amongst young people. What do you think are the advantages and disadvantages of reality TV?

DON'T FORGET

Try to pick out phrases you could use in your performance about the advantages and disadvantages of watching reality TV when reading the text on page 37.

ACTIVITY: FOR OR AGAINST REALITY TV – POUR OU CONTRE LA TÉLÉ-RÉALITÉ

Read the conversation between Mathieu and Lucie and answer the questions below. Here are some tips for how to approach a reading comprehension as part of the Unit and Course assessments.

- Start by reading the background information as this will tell you what the text is about.

- Read the questions carefully.

- The answers usually come in the same order as the questions, so the questions might also give you an idea of what the text is about.

- Pick out key words from the questions and use these to predict key words that you might see in the text.

- Look at the number of marks given for each question so you know how much information to give in your answers.

- When you read a word that you don't understand, try to make links with English words, refer to the glossary or use your dictionary to look up what they mean.

contd

Mathieu and Lucie

M: Salut Lucie, est-ce que tu as vu l'émission qui s'appelle 'Secret Story' hier soir? C'était génial. Ça m'a fait beaucoup rire et je l'ai trouvé vraiment divertissante.

L: Non, j'ai horreur des émissions de télé-réalité. La télé-réalité est devenue plus populaire depuis quelques années. Elle n'apporte rien d'utile pour la société. En plus, il est difficile d'échapper aux émissions de télé-réalité car il y en a trop.

M: Je ne suis pas d'accord. Les téléspectateurs la trouvent captivante. En effet mes parents disent que je suis accro. Selon moi, il s'agit d'un concours où les gens ont envie de gagner beaucoup d'argent ou de devenir célèbres. On voudrait réaliser son rêve, comme devenir chanteur célèbre et de temps en temps il y a des gens avec beaucoup de talent. Souvent ce sont les gens ordinaires qui participent aux emissions de télé-réalité. Je vote toujours pour les participants que je préfère.

L: Est-ce que tu plaisantes? Est-ce que tu ne te rends pas compte que c'est totalement faux, ce n'est pas la réalité. Ce que je n'aime pas, c'est que parfois les candidats font des choses choquantes et gênantes. Je pense que la télé-réalité a une mauvaise influence sur les jeunes. Les jeunes croient qu'on ne doit pas travailler dur au lycée car ils peuvent devenir riches rapidement grâce aux émissions de télé-réalité. Ça leur donne l'impression qu'il suffit de participer à une émission de télé-réalité pour être célèbre et pour être riche. Il y a des gens qui contribuent à la société en faisant beaucoup de choses pour aider les autres et à mon avis ce sont eux qui devraient recevoir de l'argent et de la publicité, pas les participants d'une emission bête.

M: Pour moi, le plus intéressant c'est observer la vie de gens et leur relations avec les autres. A mon avis on peut mieux comprendre la nature humaine en regardant ce genre d'émission. Ce que j'aime le plus, c'est que ces émissions me donnent l'espoir que ma vie peut changer facilement aussi. Peut-être que je vais m'inscrire à la prochaine série de 'Secret Story'.

Questions

1. Why did Mathieu enjoy watching the programme 'Secret Story'? (2)
2. How does Lucie describe reality TV? (2)
3. Why does she think it is difficult to escape reality TV programmes? (1)
4. What does Mathieu say the programmes are about? (1)
5. What does Mathieu always do? (1)
6. What does Lucie not like and why? (1)
7. What does Lucie say about reality TV and young people? (3)
8. According to Lucie, what do young people believe? (2)
9. Who does Lucie say deserves publicity and money? (1)
10. What does Mathieu find interesting about these programmes? (2)

ONLINE

Check out the BrightRED Digital Zone for the answers to all the activities in this section: www.brightredbooks.net/N5French

DON'T FORGET

When giving your opinion on something, always try to give a reason, introducing it with *car, parce que* or *pour* + infinitive.

DON'T FORGET

Make use of the Glossary at the back of the book if you need to check the meaning of any of the words here.

ONLINE TEST

Take the 'Reality TV – La télé-réalité' test online at www.brightredbooks.net/N5French

THINGS TO DO AND THINK ABOUT

Using the text, pick out some phrases that reflect how you feel about reality TV. Write a paragraph on reality TV. Don't forget to use **opinion phrases** and **conjunctions**. You may wish to use this paragraph in your Performance.

TECHNOLOGY – LA TECHNOLOGIE

Technology has a huge part to play in our daily lives, from using your mobile phone to using the internet to shop for clothes. How many different forms of technology do you use regularly? Here are a few to help you get started:

L'accès sans fil à internet

La messagerie électronique

Un blog

La technologie

Mettre en ligne

Un lecteur MP3

L'iPad et l'iPod

Un portable

Un ordinateur

Un SMS

⚙ ACTIVITY: USE OF TECHNOLOGY – L'USAGE DE LA TECHNOLOGIE

It would be useful to be able to say how you use technology. Read the following phrases, put them into the first person (the *je* form) and translate them into English. The first one has been put into first person for you.

Listen to the phrases online to help you with the pronunciation.

- Envoyer des SMS/des textos à ses amis avec son portable – J'envoie des SMS/des textos à mes amis avec mon portable
- Réserver des places de concerts en ligne
- Pouvoir télécharger des films et de la musique
- Faire de la recherche pour ses devoirs
- Prendre des photos avec son portable
- Commander des livres en ligne
- Surfer le net pour trouver les renseignements
- Envoyer des émails
- Utiliser Internet pour écouter de la musique ou regarder des films
- Tchater dans les forums pour rencontrer des amis
- Faire du shopping en ligne
- Rester en contact avec ses cousins à l'étranger grâce au net
- Retirer de l'argent au distributeur automatique
- Acheter les billets d'avion et réserver un hôtel pour les vacances sur le net
- Jouer à des jeux en ligne

DON'T FORGET ➕

Use a dictionary to check any verbs that you are unfamiliar with.

ACTIVITY: ADVANTAGES AND DISADVANTAGES OF TECHNOLOGY – LES AVANTAGES ET LES INCONVÉNIENTS DE LA TECHNOLOGIE

There are many advantages and disadvantages of using technology.

First, read the following phrases and try to work out what they mean before listening to them on CD. Use a dictionary to look up any unfamiliar vocabulary.

Then listen to the phrases online and put them under the correct heading of either *Avantages* or *Inconvénients*.

Finally, note down the reason(s) why they are advantages or disadvantages.

Transcript

1. La vie de tous les jours est plus facile grâce à la technologie. Je ne sais pas ce que je ferais sans mon portable. Je peux rester en contact avec mes amis et mes parents de n'importe où.

2. Selon moi, avoir un portable coûte très cher et c'est une perte d'argent. En plus l'utilisation du téléphone portable peut être dangereuse pour la santé. Les portables, ce n'est pas mon truc.

3. J'adore le monde virtuel. Je suis un vrai internaute car je fais tout sur le net. J'achète mes vêtements, je télécharge la musique et les films en ligne, ce qui est moins cher qu'acheter les CDs et les DVDs.

4. Pour moi, la technologie, c'est formidable. Mon site préféré, c'est le Facebook car je peux communiquer avec mes amis. C'est très rapide et on peut y voir les photos de ses amis immédiatement. On peut aussi exprimer ses idées et ses opinions.

5. Je pense que les sites communautaires peuvent être dangereux car on peut rencontrer des gens bizarres quand on tchate en ligne. Il y a des gens menaçants qui se cachent derrière leurs écrans.

6. Je passe des heures à trouver les produits en ligne car il y a plus de choix sur le net que dans les magasins. En plus je peux comparer les prix et acheter les produits les moins chers.

7. Je suis technophobe. Je déteste les ordinateurs car ils sont compliqués. Je ne comprends pas le langage de technologie.

8. Il existe des dangers sur le net. Les parents s'inquiètent pour la sécurité de leurs enfants car les jeunes peuvent être victimes d'intimidation sur le net.

9. On dépend trop de son téléphone portable et en effet, certains disent qu'ils ne pourraient pas survivre sans leur portable. On envoie des SMS et des messages électroniques, on parle aux amis, on lit des livres, on surfe sur le net, on joue à des jeux et on écoute de la musique. On passe trop de temps sur son portable et par conséquent, il y a moins de communication entre les personnes.

10. Ce que j'aime le plus, c'est que je peux écouter de la musique sur mon iPod sans déranger personne. Je peux aussi lire des livres en tout genre sur le même écran avec mon Kindle, ce qui est génial.

Try out Activity 1 in the end of chapter activities on the BrightRED Digital Zone for a great translation exercise about using the internet.

THINGS TO DO AND THINK ABOUT

Choose five phrases to describe how you use technology. Try to include three advantages and three disadvantages of using technology. You may wish to learn them for your Performance and you could also use them as part of your writing about leisure and hobbies.

ONLINE TEST

Why not try the 'Technology – La technologie' test at www.brightredbooks.net/N5French?

YOUR HOME AREA AS A TOURIST AREA – TA REGION COMME LIEU TOURISTIQUE

In this section, you will learn to describe why tourists might come to your home area. We will revise how to say where you live and then learn to say what is in your town that tourists might want to come and see.

WHERE DO YOU LIVE? – OÙ HABITES-TU?

Let's start off by saying where in Scotland you live:

J'habite à ... en Écosse.

Grammar

To say that you live in a town and in a country, you need to know the following:

J'habite à + name of place (Glasgow/Paris)
J'habite *en* + feminine country: en Écosse
J'habite *au* + masculine country: au Pays de Galles
J'habite *aux* + plural country: aux États-Unis

Now try and fill in the blanks with the correct word: *à, en, au, aux*. Use your dictionary to find out the gender of the country.

1. J'habite ___ Edimbourg.

2. J'habite ___ Pays-Bas.

3. J'habite ___ Espagne.

4. J'habite ___ Inverness.

5. J'habite ___ Portugal.

6. J'habite ___ Italie.

Le Nord
Le Nord-est
L'Ouest
Le Centre
Le Sud-ouest
Le Sud

Let's look at the points of the compass to say where in Scotland you live. Can you complete the points of the compass?

Do you live in a city or a town or in the countryside? Match the French to the English and use a dictionary to look up any unfamiliar vocabulary.

à la campagne	at the seaside
à la montagne	in town
au bord de la mer	in the outskirts/suburbs
dans une grande ville	in the mountains
dans un village	in the town centre
en ville	at the seaside
au centre-ville	in a city
en banlieue	in a village

Now complete the sentences about where you live:

- J'habite à ... (name of place)

- Ma ville/mon village se trouve dans le/l'... de l'Ecosse. (location)

- J'habite ... (town/countryside etc.)

⚙ ACTIVITY: DESCRIBING YOUR AREA – DÉCRIRE TON QUARTIER

It would be useful to be able to describe the area in which you live. Can you think of any adjectives that you could use to describe your home area? Here are a few to start off. Look up any words you are not familiar with in the dictionary. Then put the adjectives under the headings: positif/négatif.

- agréable
- amusant(e)
- animé(e)
- beau/belle
- ancien(ne)
- historique
- industriel(le)
- joli(e)
- magnifique
- moderne
- pittoresque
- pollué(e)
- propre
- touristique
- tranquille

⚙ ACTIVITY

Listen to the following texts online and fill in the blanks using the words in the box below. Read the text first to get the gist of what it is about and try to predict what you are going to hear.

A. J'habite à Aberdeen. C'est une _____ _____ qui se trouve dans le _____ de l'Écosse. Je pense que c'est une ville _____, dynamique et _____ .

B. J'habite à West Linton. C'est un _____ _____ qui est situé près d'Édimbourg dans le _____ de l'Écosse. Je trouve que, c'est un village historique, _____ et pittoresque.

C. J'habite à Girvan. C'est une ville moyenne qui se trouve __ __ __ __ __ ___ dans le _____ de l'Écosse. Je pense que c'est une ville ____, jolie et _____.

> au bord de la mer   petit village   touristique   industriel   propre
> grande ville   animé   nord-est   centre   sud-ouest   tranquille

✔ ONLINE TEST

Take the 'Your home area as a tourist area – Ton quartier comme lieu touristique' test online at www.brightredbooks.net/N5French

⚠ THINGS TO DO AND THINK ABOUT

Can you write a short paragraph to describe exactly where you live and what it is like? Use the language in this section to help you. You may wish to use this as part of your writing and Performance.

A TOURIST TOWN – UNE VILLE TOURISTIQUE

Can you think of what tourists visiting your home area might like to do? Think about the following:

Qu'est-ce qu'on peut faire dans ta ville? What can you do in your town?

⚙ ACTIVITY: MY TOWN – MA VILLE

Read the following texts and answer the questions. You should look for key words and verbs that will help you to identify why their home area is a good place for tourists to visit. Try to give as much information as possible in your answers.

Philippe

J'habite dans une petite ville pittoresque. En été, il y a plein de touristes qui visitent notre ville car elle se trouve au bord de la mer. On peut se promener à la plage et se balader dans la ville pour voir de beaux bâtiments. C'est un endroit idéal pour les jeunes actifs qui adorent faire des sports aquatiques. On peut faire de la planche à voile et de la plongée. En plus, on peut louer des bateaux, ce qui est vraiment amusant. Il y a des auberges de jeunesse où on peut loger pendant son séjour. En plus, il y a quelques petits restaurants typiques qui sont très populaires car la nourriture y est délicieuse.

1. Where does Philippe live? (2)

2. Name any three things that tourists can do when they visit his town in summer. (3)

3. Where can they stay in the town? (1)

4. What does he say is popular and why? (2)

Sandrine

J'habite dans une grande ville animée qui est célèbre parmi les touristes car il y a beaucoup de choses à faire et à voir. Tout d'abord, on peut visiter un grand château ancien et il y a aussi beaucoup de monuments historiques. Si on aime l'histoire ou les œuvres d'art, il y a un grand choix de musées et de galeries où on peut y passer des heures. Le soir, on peut voir des spectacles au théâtre ou on peut aller aux concerts. L'activité la plus populaire pour les touristes, c'est découvrir des monuments à bord d'un bus touristique qui fait le tour de la ville. Pour les enfants, il y a un bowling, une patinoire et un grand parc public. En plus, il y a beaucoup d'hôtels de quatre et cinq étoiles et des appartements de luxe qu'on peut louer.

1. Where does Sandrine live? (1)

2. Why is it famous amongst tourists? (1)

contd

3. Name three places that you can visit there. (3)

4. What can you do in the evening? (2)

5. What is the most popular activity amongst tourists? (1)

6. What three places does Sandrine say would be good for children? (3)

7. Where can tourists stay? (2)

Jean-Luc

Mon village se trouve à la montagne. C'est assez petit mais c'est bien connu parmi les touristes à cause des montagnes. Si on aime faire de la randonnée, mon village est l'endroit idéal. En hiver, quand il neige, on peut faire du ski. J'ai de la chance d'y habiter car le ski, c'est mon sport préféré. On peut loger dans un petit hôtel de trois étoiles, qui est situé dans la rue principale. On peut manger dans les pubs et il y a aussi un restaurant traditionnel. Malheureusement, ce que je n'aime pas c'est qu'il n'y a pas beaucoup de choses à faire le soir car il n'y a pas de cinéma ou de théâtre. Pourtant en été il y a des gens qui viennent d'autres pays pour aller aux festivals et aux fêtes de musique traditionnelle qui ont lieu près de mon village, ce qui est génial.

1. Where does Jean-Luc live? (2)

2. What can you do in the area? (2)

3. Where can you stay? (1)

4. Where can you eat? (2)

5. What does he not like about where he lives? (1)

6. What happens in the summer? (2)

DON'T FORGET

For more activities, look at the section on sports and hobbies on page 23.

Marie-Claire

J'habite en banlieue d'une grande ville dynamique et multiculturelle. Ce que j'aime le plus, c'est qu'il y a plein de touristes qui visitent ma ville pendant toute l'année et il y a une atmosphère animée. Les touristes aiment faire les magasins, acheter des souvenirs et manger dans de bons restaurants traditionnels. On peut aussi faire du tourisme car il y a également plein de sites touristiques. Si on veut voir un peu de la région, on peut visiter les lacs, les montagnes et les distilleries écossaises. En plus, on peut se déplacer facilement car il y a un bon système de transport en commun. Finalement, il y a un bon choix d'hébergement, comme les hôtels, les auberges de jeunesse et les pensions où on peut loger.

1. Where does Marie-Claire live? (3)

2. What does she like the most about her town? (2)

3. Name any three things tourists can do in Marie Claire's city. (3)

4. What can you visit in the region? (3)

5. What does she say about transport? (2)

6. Where can you stay? (3)

DON'T FORGET

Il y a un musée means 'there is a museum' and *il n'y a pas de cinéma* means 'there isn't a cinema'. *Il n'y a pas* is followed by *de*.

ONLINE TEST

Take the 'A tourist town – Une ville touristique' test online at www. brightredbooks.net/N5French

THINGS TO DO AND THINK ABOUT

Using the language in this unit, write a paragraph about what there is for tourists to do in your home area. Think about it in terms of location, activities, accommodation and eating out. You can learn this and you may wish to use it as part of your Performance.

TOWN AND COUNTRY – LA VILLE ET LA CAMPAGNE 1

In this section, we will compare life in a town or city to life in the countryside. Can you think of any obvious differences between the different ways of life?

DESCRIPTION OF THE TOWN AND THE COUNTRYSIDE – LA DESCRIPTION DE LA VILLE ET DE LA CAMPAGNE

Have a look at the following adjectives. Do you recognise any of them? If there are any unfamiliar words, look up their meaning in the dictionary and then decide if the words best describe life in the town or in the countryside. Could they be used to describe both areas?

- Tranquille
- Cosmopolite
- Calme
- Beau/belle
- Pollué(e)

- Reposant(e)
- Stressant(e)
- Animé(e)
- Ennuyeux/ennuyeuse
- Divertissant(e)

- Vert(e)
- Bruyant(e)
- Isolé(e)
- Cher/chère
- Sale

 ACTIVITY: THE TOWN – LA VILLE

We will now focus on life in a town or a city.

Read the following phrases and try to work out what the words mean by identifying familiar vocabulary. Try to work out the meaning of unfamiliar French vocabulary by making links to English words. Translate the phrases into English using a bilingual dictionary. List the phrases as either advantages or disadvantages of living in a town/city.

- C'est bruyant.
- Il y a beaucoup de pollution.
- Il y a beaucoup de choses à faire et à voir.
- On peut faire du tourisme en visitant les monuments historiques et les sites touristiques.
- Il y a beaucoup de déchets par terre.
- Il y a un bon choix de restaurants.
- Il y a trop de circulation.
- On peut faire les magasins au centre-ville.
- La vie nocturne est géniale.
- On peut sortir en boîte de nuit.

- Il y a beaucoup de moyens de faire du sport.
- Il y a trop de monde.
- Les loyers sont chers.
- On peut se déplacer facilement grâce aux transports en commun.
- Il n'y a pas assez d'espaces verts.
- Il y a plein de divertissements pour les jeunes.
- La vie peut être stressante.
- On peut profiter de la vie culturelle comme le théâtre et les musées.
- On ne connaît pas ses voisins.
- On ne se sent pas en sécurité.

 ACTIVITY: THE COUNTRYSIDE – LA CAMPAGNE

We will now do the same exercise for the countryside.

Read the French phrases and try to work out what they mean by making links to English or using a bilingual dictionary. Translate the phrases into English (good practice for Higher French!). List the phrases as either advantages or disadvantages of living in the countryside.

contd

- On est isolé.
- Il n'y a rien à faire pour les jeunes.
- Le paysage est vraiment beau.
- Il faut avoir une voiture pour se déplacer.
- Le mode de vie est reposant.
- Tout le monde se connaît.
- La vie peut être ennuyeuse et monotone.
- Il faut aller en ville pour étudier car il n'y a pas de lycées ou d'universités.
- On n'est pas pressé.
- Il n'y a pas de distractions.
- Il y a plein d'espaces verts.
- C'est assez propre.

- C'est tranquille et paisible.
- Il n'y a pas de commodités à proximité.
- L'air est pur car il y a moins de pollution.
- On peut faire de longues promenades.
- On peut se détendre.
- On vit près de la nature.
- Il y a peu de possibilités de trouver un bon emploi.
- Il y a moins de violence.
- On habite loin de ses amis.
- Tout le monde s'intéresse trop à la vie des autres.
- Il y a moins de bruit.
- Les transports en commun ne sont pas efficaces.

GRAMMAR: COMPARATIVES AND SUPERLATIVES

In this section, you have been comparing the town to the countryside. You will have noticed phrases like:

- il y a *moins* de pollution
- la vie à la campagne est *plus* reposante *que* la vie en ville
- ce que j'aime *le plus* ...

In English we can compare things by putting 'er' at the end of an adjective (smaller, taller) or by saying something is 'the _____est' (e.g. the smallest, the tallest). In French we use the following to compare things:

- plus ... (que)   more ... (than)
- moins ... (quc)   less ... (than)
- aussi ... (que)   just as ... (as)
- le/la/les plus ...   the most ...
- le/la/les moins ...   the least ...

For example:

- John est petit   John is small.
- Peter est plus petit (que John).   Peter is smaller (than John).
- Peter est aussi petit que Jacques.   Peter is as small as Jacques.
- Jack est *le* plus petit.   Jack is the smallest.
- Marie est *la* plus peti**te**.   Marie is the smallest.

Be careful, as there are some exceptions:

Adjective	Comparative	Superlative
bon(ne)(s)(nes) (good)	meilleur(e)(s)(es) (better)	le/la/les meilleur(e)(s)(es) (the best)
mauvais(e)(es) (bad)	pire(s) (worse)	le/la/les pire(s) (the worst)

For example:

- Le café est meilleur que le thé.   Coffee is better than tea.
- Le chocolat chaud est le meilleur.   Hot chocolate is the best.

ONLINE TEST

Take the 'Prepositions' test at www.brightredbooks.net/N5French

THINGS TO DO AND THINK ABOUT

Now try to write a short paragraph about the advantages and disadvantages of living in the town and the countryside. How many of the phrases from the above sections can you remember? You may wish to use this as part of your Performance.

TOWN AND COUNTRY – LA VILLE ET LA CAMPAGNE 2

ACTIVITY: COMPARATIVE AND SUPERLATIVE

Now try to translate the following sentences using the **comparative** and **superlative**.

1. The town is more fun than the countryside.
2. The town is less boring than the countryside.
3. The town is the most fun.
4. The countryside is the most boring.
5. The town is the least boring.
6. The countryside is the least fun.
7. The town is the best.
8. The countryside is the worst.

DON'T FORGET

The adjective must agree with the gender and number of the noun that it is describing.

ACTIVITY: TOWN OR COUNTRYSIDE – LA VILLE OU LA CAMPAGNE

Read the following two texts and answer the following questions:

1. Where did each person used to live?
2. What did they like about it?
3. Where do they live now?
4. What do they like about it?
5. Where would they prefer to live if they had the choice and why?

VIDEO LINK

Have a look at 'Living in Strasbourg' at www.brightredbooks.net/N5French

Corine

Quand j'étais petite, j'habitais à la campagne. On a déménagé car mon père a trouvé un nouveau boulot. J'aimais la vie à la campagne car on connaissait tout le monde et on avait beaucoup de liberté. On pouvait jouer dehors quand il faisait beau car il y avait plein d'espaces verts. Maintenant, nous habitons dans une grande ville. Ce que j'aime le plus, c'est que tous mes amis habitent près de chez moi. Il est facile de se déplacer et il y a toujours quelque chose à faire comme aller au cinéma ou faire les magasins au centre commercial. Si j'avais le choix, j'habiterais en ville parce que la ville est plus animée que la campagne. En plus, il y a énormément de distractions pour les jeunes.

ONLINE TEST

Take the 'Town and country – La ville et la campagne' test online at www.brightredbooks.net/N5French

Bernard

Quand j'étais plus jeune, j'habitais en ville. J'aimais la vie en ville car on pouvait se déplacer facilement et il y avait beaucoup de distractions. Par contre, il y avait trop de monde, trop de pollution et trop de bruit en ville. Maintenant, nous habitons à la campagne. J'adore la vie à la campagne car il y a moins de crime et de violence donc on se sent en sécurité. En plus, j'aime vivre près de la nature et passer mon temps libre à faire des randonnées à pied. Si j'avais le choix, j'habiterais à la campagne car j'adore la tranquillité et le mode de vie paisible.

Now look at this third text about life at the seaside.

DON'T FORGET

This last text (Delphine) is an example of how the language you have learned which describes the town or countryside can be adapted to describe life at the seaside.

Delphine

Avant j'habitais dans une ville moyenne au bord de la mer. La vie était vraiment passionnante car il y avait toujours beaucoup de choses à faire. Normalement, on aimait passer le week-end à la plage. On faisait de longues promenades, on faisait des sports nautiques, comme la planche à voile ou on jouait au volley. C'était génial. On est parti de la ville quand j'avais onze ans. La vie est vraiment calme à la campagne et au début, je l'ai trouvée ennuyeuse. Je me suis habituée à la tranquillité et je dirais que maintenant, je préfère vivre à la campagne. Ce que j'aime le plus, c'est qu'il n'y a pas de touristes en été et il y a moins de circulation. À l'avenir, si j'ai le choix, j'habiterai en ville car je voudrais aller à l'université pour étudier les langues étrangères.

contd

KNOWLEDGE ABOUT LANGUAGE

What do you notice about the verbs in the three reading texts? Can you spot the different tenses that we have already learned?

Can you spot the verbs in the present tense? Refer to page 7 to revise the present tense.

Can you pick out verbs in the perfect tense? Refer to pages 67–9 to revise the perfect tense.

Can you pick out verbs in the imperfect tense? Refer to page 45 to revise the imperfect tense.

What about the future and conditional tenses? Refer to page 86 to revise the future and conditional tenses.

DON'T FORGET

Look for time phrases to help you identify the different tenses, for example *maintenant* indicates an action happening in the present tense while *à l'avenir* refers to actions happening in the future.

GRAMMAR: THE IMPERFECT TENSE – L'IMPARFAIT

Take another look at the sections which describe where each person used to live and see if you can work out a pattern. The tense used is called the imperfect tense or l'imparfait.

We use the imperfect tense:
- to describe a past repeated action
- to describe what something or someone *was* like in the past
- to say what someone *used to do*

How do we form the imperfect tense?
1. Start with the 'nous' form of the verb in the present tense.
2. Take off the '-ons' to form the stem.
3. Add the imperfect ending.

je jou*ais*	I used to play/was playing
tu jou*ais*	you used to play/were playing
il jou*ait*	he used to play/was playing
elle jou*ait*	she used to play/was playing
on jou*ait*	we used to play/were playing

- to describe an interrupted action in the past – to say what someone/something was doing when something else happened.

e.g. Jouer– to play.
1. Start with the 'nous' part in the present tense: *nous jouons.*
2. Take off '-ons': *jou.*
3. Add endings:

nous jou*ions*	we used to play/were playing
vous jou*iez*	you used to play/were playing
ils jou*aient*	they used to play/were playing
elles jou*aient*	they used to play/were playing

You will be pleased to know that there is only one irregular verb in the imperfect tense, être – it uses the same endings, but the stem is 'ét':

j'étais	I was/used to be
tu étais	you were/used to be
il etait	he was/used to be
elle était	she was/used to be
on était	we were/used to be

nous étions	we were/used to be
vous étiez	you were/used to be
ils étaient	they were/used to be
elles étaient	they were/used to be

Try the end of chapter activities on the Digital Zone for extra practice on the imperfect tense.

THINGS TO DO AND THINK ABOUT

- Make up a paragraph about where you used to live and what you liked or didn't like (it doesn't have to be true!).
- Then describe where you live now give your opinions about what you think of it and reasons for your opinions.
- To finish, say where you would like to live.

This is your chance to show how good you are so try to use different tenses, time phrases, linking words, comparatives, superlatives and opinion phrases. You may wish to use this as part of your Performance.

ENVIRONMENT – L'ENVIRONNEMENT

Can you think of different ways that you can be environmentally friendly at home? Here are a few to help you get started:

Réutiliser les sacs en plastiques

Utiliser les produits verts

Faire du recyclage

L'environnement

Aller à pied

Eteindre la lumière

Réduire les déchets

⚙ ACTIVITY: PROBLEMS WITH OUR ENVIRONMENT – LES PROBLÈMES DE L'ENVIRONNEMENT

Let's start off by looking at the environmental problems that we are faced with. Read the phrases and translate them into English. Can you work out what they mean by making links to English phrases to do with environmental problems? If there are any phrases you are unsure of, use a bilingual dictionary to look them up.

1. La déforestation
2. Le réchauffement de la terre et le changement climatique
3. La pollution de l'air à cause des véhicules
4. La circulation et les embouteillages
5. La sécheresse
6. L'extinction des espèces menacées
7. L'effet de serre et le trou dans la couche d'ozone
8. La pluie acide à cause des activités industrielles
9. Les déchets
10. L'emballage
11. Le gaspillage d'énergie
12. La pollution de l'eau

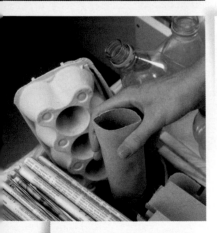

⚙ ACTIVITY: PROTECTING THE ENVIRONMENT – PROTÉGER L'ENVIRONNEMENT

Read through the following ways to help to protect our environment and translate them into English. Then match them to the problems above.

1. Il faut utiliser l'essence sans plomb.
2. Il faut protéger les espèces menacées, par exemple les animaux qui habitent dans les forêts tropicales.
3. Il faut aller à pied ou utiliser les transports en commun.
4. Il faut planter des arbres.
5. Il faut limiter l'utilisation des CFC.
6. On doit trier les déchets pour recycler le papier, le plastique et le verre.
7. Il faut réduire la consommation d'eau en fermant le robinet et en prenant une douche au lieu d'un bain.
8. Il faut utiliser les énergies renouvelables et réduire la production de gaz carbonique.
9. Il faut réduire les déchets et éviter le gaspillage.
10. Il faut éviter de jeter les ordures dans la mer.
11. Il faut réduire les émissions des usines et la consommation de combustibles fossiles.
12. Il faut conserver l'énergie et utiliser plus d'énergies propres et renouvelables, comme l'énergie solaire, l'énergie éolienne ou hydroulique.

DON'T FORGET ✚

Il faut is a useful phrase meaning 'we must' or 'it is necessary to' and it is always followed by the infinitive.

ACTIVITY: MODAL VERBS – LES VERBES MODAUX

Have a go at Activity 4 in the end of chapter activities (on the BrightRED Digital Zone), which will help you with the next exercise.

Following the listening activity, try to complete this task.

1. Look at the infinitives in the box below and work out what they mean.
2. Complete the sentences.
3. Try to translate the sentences – this will be good practice for Higher French!

Only look at the text from the listening if you get stuck, otherwise use your common sense to fill in the blanks with the appropriate verb.

1. Il faut _____ les matériaux recyclables, comme les journaux, le verre et le plastique.
2. On doit _____ du papier recyclé et des piles rechargeables au supermarché.
3. On devrait _____ les sacs en plastique.
4. On pourrait _____ _____ la consommation d'eau.
5. On peut _____ les produits écologiques à la maison.
6. On devrait _____ à pied ou en transport en commun.
7. Il faut _____ les lumières quand on quitte une pièce.
8. On ne devrait pas _____ l'énergie.
9. On doit _____ l'environnement.
10. Au lieu de _____ un bain, il faut se doucher.

acheter	prendre	réduire	éteindre	gaspiller	recycler	aller	protéger
	réutiliser	utiliser					

 THINGS TO DO AND THINK ABOUT

Write a short essay about what you and your family do to help the environment. Try to use some of the opening sentences and conjunctions from Activity 4 in the end of chapter activities (www.brightredbooks.net/N5French). This could be used as part of your Performance. You could structure it in the following way:

Introduction: What is your short essay about? Name a few environmental problems.

Je voudrais écrire au sujet de l'environnement. De nos jours il y a des problèmes de l'environnement comme …

Paragraph 1: What environmental problems are there?

C'est vrai qu'il y a beaucoup de problèmes d'environnement. Par exemple, …

Paragraph 2: What should everyone do?

Il faut/Il ne faut pas/On doit/On ne doit pas/On devrait/On ne devrait pas/On peut + infinitive

Paragraph 3: What you do:

Je …/Ma famille …/Mes parents … (see the phrases used in the listening transcript from Activity 4 in the end of chapter activities on the Digital Zone)

Conclusion:

En somme, il est important de protéger notre planète.

 ONLINE

Before you complete this activity, try out Activity 4 in the end of chapter activities at www.brightredbooks.net/N5French

 DON'T FORGET

On doit and *on devrait* come from the verb *devoir*, meaning 'to have to' or 'must', and *on peut* and *on pourrait* come from the verb *pouvoir*, meaning 'to be able to' or 'can'. Modal verbs are always followed by the infinitive.

 VIDEO LINK

Watch the clips 'Le recyclage au Canada' and 'Protéger l'eau' at www.brightredbooks.net/N5French

 ONLINE TEST

Take the 'Environment – L'environnement' test online at www.brightredbooks.net/N5French

LEARNING

SCHOOL SUBJECTS – LES MATIÈRES

In this chapter we will look at the context of learning. The topics we will cover include:

- Learning activities you enjoy
- Learning activities you don't enjoy
- Preparing for exams
- Comparing education systems in Scotland to other systems
- How to improve education systems

ONLINE TEST

Take the test 'School subjects – Les matières' at www.brightredbooks.net/N5French.

REVISION – LA REVISION

At this stage, it would be worth revising school subjects. How many can you remember off the top of your head?

 ACTIVITY: LEARNING ACTIVITIES – LES ACTIVITÉS D'APPRENTISSAGE

Think about the range of activities you do in each subject. Can you work out what the following activities mean in English?

1. Apprendre le vocabulaire
2. Résoudre les problèmes
3. Travailler tout(e) seul(e)
4. Travailler en groupe/en équipe
5. Travailler à deux
6. Travailler à l'ordinateur
7. Copier les notes du tableau
8. Regarder les documentaires
9. Lire
10. Chercher les mots dans le dictionnaire
11. Faire des recherches
12. Rédiger des dissertations
13. Créer
14. Dessiner
15. Faire les devoirs
16. Faire des présentations
17. Jouer des instruments
18. Faire des activités sportives
19. Participer aux jeux
20. Écouter le prof

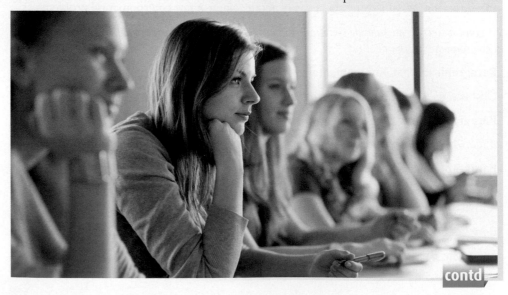

contd

21. Communiquer avec ses camarades de classe

22. Faire de l'arithmétique et de l'algèbre

23. Faire des travaux manuels comme le bricolage

24. Cuisiner

25. Apprendre la grammaire

26. Apprendre l'orthographe

27. Passer les examens (oraux/écrits)

28. Faire des expériences scientifiques

 ACTIVITY: SUBJECTS AND ACTIVITIES – LES MATIÈRES ET LES ACTIVITÉS

1. Write a list in French of the subjects you are currently studying at school.

2. Beside each subject write at least one activity that you do in this subject. Try to put the infinitives into the 'je' form (refer to page 7 if you need to revise how to form the present tense). Look up the verb section in your dictionary to check any irregular verbs.

 ACTIVITY: WHAT DO YOU LIKE DOING AT SCHOOL/ COLLEGE OR UNIVERSITY? – QU'EST-CE QUE TU AIMES FAIRE AU LYCÉE/À LA FAC?

Now that you have decided which activities you do in different subjects, you will learn how to give your opinion of the different activities. Refer to page 25 to revise opinion phrases before you start this exercise.

Listen to the following four people discussing what they like and dislike doing at school and complete the table below. Write as much as you can under each heading (you may need to use extra paper).

 DON'T FORGET

When giving your opinion in French remember that phrases like *j'aime, j'adore, je n'aime pas, je déteste* and *je préfère* are all followed by the verb in the infinitive, for example *j'aime travailler* means 'I like to work', but often in English we translate it as 'I like working'.

Name	Subject	Activities they enjoy	Reason	Activities they dislike	Reason
Frédéric					
Corinne					
Thierry					
Anna					

 THINGS TO DO AND THINK ABOUT

Can you write about some of the learning activities you do at school? Try to include:

- which activities you do in different subjects

- which activities you enjoy

- which activities you do not enjoy.

Don't forget to give reasons for your opinions. You may wish to use this as part of your Performance.

 VIDEO LINK

Check out the clip 'Les cours et les devoirs' at www. brightredbooks.net/N5French

PREPARING FOR EXAMS 1 – SE PREPARER AUX EXAMENS

As you are using this book, it is likely you are preparing for your French exams. In this section we will look at different types of exams and how best to prepare for them.

DON'T FORGET

Passer mes examens is a false friend meaning 'to sit an exam', not 'to pass an exam' and *assister à* means 'to attend', not 'to assist'.

DON'T FORGET

Je suis en train de + infinitive means 'I am in the middle of doing' something. It is a fancy phrase that you could use in different contexts.

PASSER LES EXAMENS – TO SIT EXAMS

Let's start by thinking about how you might introduce talking about your exams. We all strive to do well and, by getting good grades in your exams, you will have a lot of opportunities open to you. We will start by saying what exams you are sitting and that you need to work hard this year to succeed. Can you work out what the following phrases mean?

- Cette année je passe mes examens de National 5.
- J'étudie six matières, y compris les maths, l'anglais, le français, l'histoire, la musique et la biologie.
- Je suis en train de me préparer aux examens de National 5.
- Je vais passer mes examens de National 5 à la fin de l'année scolaire.
- Je voudrais réussir à mes examens cette année car j'ai l'intention de continuer mes études l'année prochaine.
- Si j'ai de bonnes notes, je pourrai trouver un bon emploi à l'avenir.
- Je dois beaucoup travailler pour réussir à mes examens.
- Je dois travailler dur(e) pour réussir à mes examens car j'ai envie de quitter le lycée et trouver un bon emploi.

At this point, you could link why you want to do well in your exams to your future plans. Refer to the section on future plans on page 72.

ACTIVITY: THE EXAMS – LES EXAMENS

Now look at the different types of tasks that you might have to do as part of your exams. Can you work out what they mean in English? You could try to guess which subject(s) each phrase refers to.

1. J'ai des examens écrits et oraux.
2. Je dois passer des examens d'écoute.
3. Je dois lire des textes.
4. Je dois faire des présentations.
5. Je dois répondre aux questions.
6. Il faut rédiger des dissertations.
7. Il faut faire des expériences.
8. Il faut faire de l'arithmétique.
9. Il faut cuisiner un repas.
10. Je dois jouer de la guitare/Je dois chanter.
11. Je dois dessiner des images.
12. Je dois faire du bricolage.
13. Il faut résoudre des problèmes.
14. Il faut pratiquer du sport.
15. Il faut travailler à l'ordinateur.

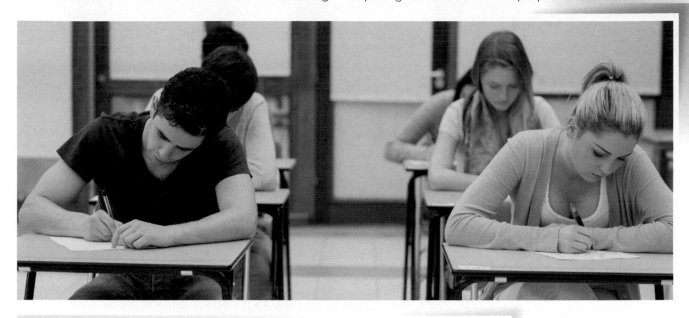

ACTIVITY: PREPARATIONS – LES PRÉPARATIONS

What preparation do you do for your different exams? Match the French phrases to the English translations:

French	English
J'assiste aux cours	I learn useful words and definitions off by heart
Je m'entraîne à l'examen de français	I do research
Je révise en ligne	I spend a lot of time doing revision at home
J'utilise des sites pour la révision sur Internet	I go to extra classes
Je fais de la recherche	I attend lessons
Je lis mes notes	I practise for the French exam
J'apprends des mots utiles et les définitions par cœur	I do revision online
Je passe beaucoup de temps à réviser chez moi	I read my notes
Je vais aux cours supplémentaires	If there are things I don't understand, I ask my teacher to explain
J'ai un emploi du temps pour réviser	I have a revision timetable
S'il y a des choses que je ne comprends pas, je demande à mon prof de m'expliquer	I use websites to do revision

 ONLINE TEST

For more false friends try the test at www.brightredbooks.net/N5French

 ONLINE

Check out the French Exam Skills page to prepare yourself ahead of your National 5 examination: www.brightredbooks.net/N5French

 THINGS TO DO AND THINK ABOUT

Look back at the phrases above. Try to think of three further sentences in French about things you do to prepare for exams. You could refer back to the sections on leisure and healthy living and use some phrases from there to help you out.

PREPARING FOR EXAMS 2 – SE PREPARER AUX EXAMENS

ACTIVITY: THE PRESSURE OF EXAMS – LA PRESSION DES EXAMENS

Read the following texts and then answer the questions below.

Benjamin

En ce moment j'étudie pour mes examens. Je trouve qu'il y a beaucoup de pression et mes parents sont toujours sur mon dos. C'est vraiment difficile car je ne suis pas très travailleur et je préférerais passer mon temps à surfer le net ou à jouer aux jeux en ligne. Pour moi, il est important de trouver l'équilibre entre les études et les loisirs pourtant mes parents ne sont pas d'accord. Ils disent que je dois étudier pendant des heures sans faire de pause, mais je trouve les révisions insupportables et vraiment ennuyeuses. Après avoir passé mes examens, j'ai envie de quitter le lycée et de trouver un emploi. Je n'ai pas l'intention de continuer mes études au lycée.

Laure

Cette année, je me prépare pour mes examens. Je sais que c'est ma responsabilité parce que j'ai l'intention de continuer mes études à la fac, donc je dois réussir à mes examens. Ça peut être stressant mais je sais que ce n'est que pour quelques mois. Je ne sors pas assez souvent avec mes amis car je me consacre à mes études. Je sais qu'il est important de bien dormir, de faire des pauses et de bien manger car on peut mieux se concentrer si on se sent bien. Mes parents me soutiennent et ils savent que je fais de mon mieux.

1. Who is not coping well with the pressure of exams?

2. Who is taking responsibility for their exams?

3. Who is working hard?

4. Who would prefer to be on the computer instead of studying?

5. Whose parents are very supportive?

6. Whose parents are putting them under a lot of pressure?

7. Who is not going to continue studying?

8. Who wants to go to university?

9. Who doesn't see their friends much?

10. Who studies for hours without taking a break?

11. Who thinks that being healthy will help them to concentrate?

contd

Now find the French for the following in the texts:

1. There is a lot of pressure.
2. It's my responsibility.
3. My parents are always on my back.
4. I have to pass my exams.
5. I would prefer to spend my free time ...
6. To find the balance between studies and leisure ...
7. Exams are unbearable.
8. It can be stressful.
9. I devote myself to my studies.
10. I don't intend to continue.
11. You can concentrate better if you feel well.
12. I am doing my best.

THINGS TO DO AND THINK ABOUT

There may be some phrases in the text that you may wish to use in your Performance. Write a paragraph about:

- your ambitions to do well in your exams
- the exams you are working towards
- what exactly you have to do
- how you prepare for your exams
- whether you think you are coping well with the pressure.

VIDEO LINK

Watch the clip 'Jobs, study and qualifications' and try out the listening comprehension exercise at the end: www.brightredbooks.net/N5French

ONLINE TEST

Try the 'Preparing for exams' test at www.brightredbooks.net/N5French

DON'T FORGET

Après avoir and *après être* are known as the **perfect infinitive** and they translate as 'after having done something', for example *après avoir passé mes examens* means 'after having sat my exams'. They are followed by the past participle and the agreement rules for *être* verbs apply.

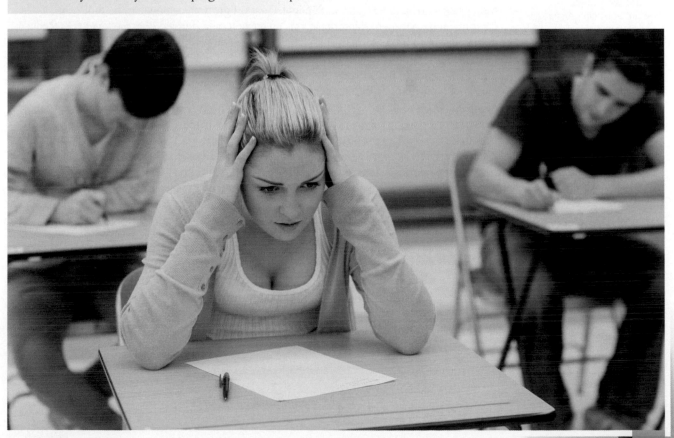

DIFFERENT EDUCATION SYSTEMS – LES SYSTÈMES SCOLAIRES DIFFÉRENTS

The Scottish education system is very different from systems in other countries.

ONLINE

To find out more about Francophone countries, why not do some research using the sites on the BrightRED Digital Zone.

DON'T FORGET

It is very important that you revise French numbers regularly. In this topic about school, you need to recognise and understand different numbers in the context of the number of pupils at school and time. Make sure you spend lots of time revising numbers!

ONLINE TEST

Head to www.brightredbooks.net/N5French and take the test on different education systems.

ACTIVITY: THE SCHOOL SYSTEM – LE SYSTÈME SCOLAIRE

Read the following texts about two young people talking about their school system then answer the questions in the table.

Isabelle

Je vais au lycée à Québec. C'est un lycée moyen avec neuf cent cinquante élèves. Le bâtiment est moderne et bien équipé. Je vais au lycée à vélo. Les cours commencent à huit heures quinze et finissent à quatorze heures quarante. Il y a quatre cours par jour et chaque cours dure une heure et quart. Il y a une récré à dix heures cinquante-cinq et le déjeuner est à midi trente. Le déjeuner dure cinquante minutes et je mange à la cantine avec mes amis. La nourriture est très saine et à mon avis, il y a un bon choix. J'étudie huit matières et ma matière préférée, c'est le dessin. Il y a vingt-cinq élèves dans ma classe et il faut aller aux salles de classe différentes, par exemple, il y a des labos et des salles d'informatique. J'aime les profs au lycée car ils sont compréhensifs et patients. Au lycée, on ne doit pas porter l'uniforme, ce qui je pense est une mauvaise idée. Je préférerais porter l'uniforme car il est cher d'acheter des vêtements différents pour être à la mode au lycée tous les jours. Ce que j'aime le plus c'est qui je peux passer du temps avec mes amis, on bavarde et on rigole pendant le déjeuner. Par contre, ce que je n'aime pas c'est qu'il n'y a pas assez de bancs dans la cour de récré.

Pierre

Mon lycée se trouve à Dakar au Sénégal. C'est un grand lycée avec mille huit cent élèves. C'est un vieux bâtiment démodé. Je vais au lycée à pied donc je dois me lever très tôt le matin car les cours commencent à 8 heures. Les cours finissent à dix-sept heures. Il y a quatre cours par jour et chaque cours dure deux heures. Nous avons une récré qui dure une demi-heure et nous avons une heure pour le déjeuner à midi. Normalement je vais chez moi pour manger le déjeuner car la cantine est trop chère. J'étudie neuf matières et ma matière préférée, c'est la géographie. Il y a quarante-sept élèves dans ma classe et nous restons dans la même salle de classe toute la journée. Il y a un terrain de foot et un terrain de basket. Les profs sont abordables et ils respectent les élèves. Le règlement au lycée est très strict, par exemple on n'a pas le droit d'utiliser des portables ou de parler pendant les cours. Ce que j'aime le plus, c'est qu'il ne faut pas porter l'uniforme donc je me sens confortable. Ce que je n'aime pas, c'est qu'il n'y a pas assez d'ordinateurs.

Questions	Isabelle	Pierre	Mélanie (listening)
Where is the school?			
What size is it?			
How many pupils are there?			
What is the building like?			
How do they get to school?			
What time do lessons start and finish?			
How many classes do they have per day and how long does each class last?			
What time is lunch?			
How long is the lunch break?			

contd

Where do they eat lunch?			
What is their opinion of the canteen?			
How many subjects do they study?			
What is their favourite subject?			
How many pupils are there in their classes?			
What facilities are there?			
What do they say about their teachers?			
Do they wear a uniform?			
What is their opinion of wearing a uniform?			
What do they like about school?			
What do they not like about school?			

ACTIVITY: MÉLANIE'S SCHOOL

Now that you have read about Isabelle's and Pierre's schools, listen to Mélanie describe her school. Use the same table as before and complete as many details as possible by listening out for key words.

ACTIVITY: THE SCHOOL SYSTEM IN SCOTLAND – LE SYSTÈME SCOLAIRE EN ÉCOSSE

Now that you have read about different school systems in different French speaking countries, it would also be a good idea to think about how these schools differ from Scottish schools. Listen to Nicolas describing the school system in Scotland. Here are some tips:

- Read the information that you are required to find (the questions/ the table) and underline key words
- Try to predict what you are going to hear (numbers/ places/ people/ activities/ times etc.)
- Think about the vocabulary that you might hear and predict the key words that you need to listen out for (bâtiment/élèves / commencent/ finissent/profs/ etc.)
- The first time you listen to the text, try to answer as many of the questions as you can but don't worry if you don't get every piece of information

- Put a star or a tick beside the questions that you didn't complete so the second time you listen to the text, you know what questions and information to focus on
- The third time you listen to the text should be your chance to fill in any remaining gaps and check the answers that you have written down are correct
- Make sure to always check your answers carefully – do they actually answer the questions?
- Don't leave any blanks, do your best to make an intelligent guess!

Questions:
1. Where is the school that Nicholas visited?
2. What size is it?
3. How many pupils are there in the school?
4. What is the building like?
5. When do classes start and finish?
6. What time is lunch?
7. What do most pupils do at lunch time?
8. How many subjects do pupils study?
9. How many pupils are in each class?
10. What does he say about pupils wearing uniform?
11. What does Nicolas like about Scottish schools?
12. What does Nicolas dislike about Scottish schools?

THINGS TO DO AND THINK ABOUT

Using the reading and listening texts in this section as a guide for structure and content, write as much as you can about your school. You can select appropriate vocabulary from the reading texts and the listening transcripts and change the key information to describe your school. You can use this text as part of your Performance.

- Where is your school?
- What is your school like?
- What size is your school?
- What time do lessons start and finish?
- How many lessons are there per day?
- How long do lessons last?
- How many pupils are in each class?
- Do you have to wear uniform?
- What is your opinion of wearing uniform?
- What do you like about your school system?
- What do you dislike about your school system?

IMPROVING EDUCATION SYSTEMS – AMÉLIORER LES SYSTÈMES SCOLAIRES

HOW CAN YOU IMPROVE YOUR EDUCATION SYSTEM? – COMMENT EST-CE QU'ON PEUT AMÉLIORER SON SYSTÈME SCOLAIRE?

We have looked at the education systems in different countries. Was there anything that you liked about the other systems that you would like to happen in your school? Think about the following:

 ACTIVITY: MY PREFERENCES AT SCHOOL – MES PRÉFÉRENCES AU LYCÉE

Have a look at the following phrases, which describe some common complaints about schools and how they would ideally be. Translate them into English then try to match the complaints to the correct ideal situation.

Common complaints	Ideal situation
Les cours sont ennuyeux.	Je voudrais porter ce que je veux au lycée.
Je trouve les matières traditionnelles assez monotones.	Je préférerais une récré d'une demi-heure.
Il y a trente élèves dans ma classe.	J'aimerais avoir plus d'équipements sportifs.
Les cours commencent à neuf heures.	Je voudrais avoir deux heures pour le déjeuner.
Les cours finissent à trois heures et demie.	Je voudrais des cours intéressants et amusants.
Nous avons quarante-cinq minutes pour le déjeuner.	Je préfère être dans une classe de vingt élèves.
On a une récré de quinze minutes.	Je voudrais étudier des matières plus dynamiques et modernes comme la danse.
C'est trop cher et il n'y a pas de choix à la cantine.	J'aimerais avoir plus de liberté au lycée.
Il n'y a pas assez d'ordinateurs.	Je voudrais finir à une heure.
Il n'y a pas assez d'équipements sportifs.	Je voudrais commencer à onze heures.
La bibliothèque est petite et il n'y a pas assez de choix de livres.	Je voudrais avoir des plats moins chers et plus de choix à la cantine.
Le règlement est trop strict.	Je préfère les profs qui sont détendus.
Les élèves n'ont pas beaucoup de liberté.	J'aimerais avoir plus de salles d'informatique.
Il faut porter un uniforme, ce qui est affreux.	J'aimerais moins de règles au lycée.
On ne doit pas porter d'uniforme.	J'aimerais avoir des profs qui ne donneraient jamais de devoirs.
Mes profs sont très sévères.	J'aimerais une grande bibliothèque avec un bon choix de livres.
Les profs nous donnent trop de devoirs.	Je voudrais porter l'uniforme car tout le monde est égal.

ACTIVITY: THE RULES – LE RÈGLEMENT

Let's focus more closely on the rules in school that you would like to change and the reasons why. Listen to the following people talking about which rules they would like to change at their school and why. Fill in the gaps using the words in the boxes below. Here are some tips to help you complete this listening task:

- Read through the texts first to get an idea of what the subject matter is and use your dictionary to look up any new words you don't recognise.

- Try to predict what you might hear by guessing in advance what words might fit into the blanks.

- Listen to the text as many times as you need to until all the gaps have been filled in.

Antoine

A mon avis, mon lycée est un _____ lycée. Il y a trop de _____ et il faut les suivre. Pendant les cours on doit _____ le prof et on n'a pas le droit de _____ ou de manger. En plus, on n'a pas le droit d'utiliser son _____ au lycée, même pendant la récré ou l'heure du déjeuner. Je pense que le règlement, ce n'est pas _____.

> boire   mauvais   juste   portable   écouter   règles

Bernadette

Au lycée, il faut porter l'uniforme. Certains pensent que c'est une _____ idée car tout le monde se _____ et donc il n'y a pas d'_____. Je pense que l'uniforme, c'est une bonne idée. Ça ne _____ pas cher et on ne peut pas remarquer les différences _____ entre les élèves. En plus, on ne _____ pas de temps à décider quoi porter chaque matin.

> coûte   individualité   perd   sociales   ressemble   mauvaise

Stéphanie

Mon lycée idéal serait assez petit et très moderne. Il n'y aurait que quinze _____ dans chaque classe et les profs seraient vraiment gentils et _____. Ils ne nous donneraient jamais de _____. Les cours commenceraient à dix heures et finiraient à une heure. On étudierait des matières intéressantes et _____. On aurait le droit d'utiliser son _____ et son iPad pendant les cours. La nourriture à la cantine serait _____ et pas chère. Il n'y aurait pas d'uniforme et on aurait le droit de porter ce qu'on veut.

> serviables   élèves   portable   devoirs   saine   utiles

What do you notice about Stéphanie's text? Do you recognise the tense she is using to describe her ideal school? Think back to the section when you described your ideal parents (pages 16–17) or your ideal place to live (pages 40–5). Can you think of any other things that you would like to change about your school or education system? Try to use the conditional tense to talk about your ideal school.

 THINGS TO DO AND THINK ABOUT

Now write a paragraph describing what happens at your school and what you would like to change. Use the phrases in this section to help you or try to make up your own. Think about the school day, your subjects, teachers, school rules, facilities, canteen and extra-curricular activities. Try to include a couple of phrases using the conditional tense. You may wish to use this paragraph as part of your Performance.

DIFFERENT JOBS – LES EMPLOIS DIFFÉREN[T]

This chapter on employability is all about the world of work. We'll start by revising different types of jobs.

```
                    Électricien(e)      Ingénieur(e)

     Pharmacien(ne)          Future          Fermier/fermière
                              jobs

            Coiffeur/coiffeuse       Infirmier/infirmière
```

DON'T FORGET

Many job names in French change depending on gender, for example *coiffeur* is masculine and *coiffeuse* is feminine. If you are unsure of the feminine form of different jobs, use your dictionary to check.

ONLINE TEST

Take the online test to revise different jobs at www.brightredbooks/N5French

ONLINE

Look at the vocabulary list online for more professions: www.brightredbooks.net/N5French

DON'T FORGET

Je suis infirmier means 'I am a nurse': in French you *do not* include the **indefinite article** (a).

⚙ ACTIVITY: WHERE DO YOU WORK? – OÙ TRAVAILLES-TU?

Look at the following phrases about places of work. Can you match the phrases to the correct job or jobs that follow?

Je travaille dans un hôpital.	Je suis infirmier.
Je travaille dans un lycée.	Je suis vendeur.
Je travaille dans une école primaire.	Je suis agent de police.
Je travaille dans un restaurant.	Je suis serveur.
Je travaille dans un garage.	Je suis secrétaire.
Je travaille dans un commissariat.	Je suis instituteur
Je travaille dans un bureau.	Je suis professeur.
Je travaille dans un magasin.	Je suis mécanicien.

ACTIVITY: QUALITIES FOR DIFFERENT JOBS – LES QUALITÉS POUR LES EMPLOIS DIFFÉRENTS

Different jobs require different qualities and skills, for example to be a teacher you need to be patient, organised and have good communication skills.

Have a look at the following phrases about skills and list them under the jobs shown that require that skill. There might be some skills that match more than one job. Use your dictionary to work out the meanings of any unfamiliar vocabulary.

Pharmacien(ne)   Journaliste   Pompier   Réceptionniste

1. Il faut être travailleur et en bonne forme.
2. On doit être motivé et déterminé.
3. Il faut être organisé et flexible.
4. On doit aimer travailler en équipe.
5. Il faut avoir de l'énergie et de l'enthousiasme.
6. Il faut avoir de bonnes notes et un diplôme.
7. On doit avoir la capacité de travailler sous la pression.
8. Il faut avoir une connaissance des ordinateurs.
9. On doit avoir une bonne mémoire.
10. On doit savoir taper rapidement.
11. Il faut savoir bien communiquer avec les autres.
12. C'est utile si on sait parler une langue étrangère.

ACTIVITY: REVISION – LA RÉVISION

1. Choose three different jobs and write down in French what skills you need for them using the vocabulary you have just learned.

2. Now translate the following paragraphs into English using all of the vocabulary from this section. Use a dictionary to help you work out the meaning of any unfamiliar language. Don't forget to make links to English where possible!

(a) Je voudrais être médecin. Il faut réussir à mes examens et je dois obtenir de bonnes notes. Pour être médecin on doit avoir de la patience, savoir bien communiquer avec les gens malades et avoir la capacité de travailler sous la pression.

(b) J'aimerais être musicienne. On doit être créatif et avoir beaucoup de talent, d'enthousiasme et d'énergie. J'aimerais savoir parler une langue étrangère car c'est utile si on a l'occasion de voyager autour du monde.

(c) À l'avenir, je voudrais devenir vétérinaire. On doit être travailleur, poli et organisé. Il faut savoir bien communiquer avec les autres et on doit adorer les animaux. En plus, il est important d'avoir une bonne mémoire.

(d) À l'avenir, j'aimerais être hôtesse de l'air. Il faut être en forme, sociable et poli. Je voudrais voyager autour du monde et j'habiterai peut-être à l'étranger. On doit travailler en équipe et aimer travailler avec le public.

THINGS TO DO AND THINK ABOUT

Using the vocabulary in this section choose a job that you would like to do in the future and write a paragraph about the qualities you need to have to do this job successfully. You will be able to add to this when we get to the section on future plans and may wish to use this as part of your Performance. You should also refer to the section on writing to help you.

DON'T FORGET

On doit and *il faut* are always followed by the infinitive. *On doit* comes from the modal verb *devoir*, and *savoir* is another modal verb meaning 'to know how to'. To revise modal verbs, look at pages 26–7.

VIDEO LINK

Check out the clips about the world of work: www.brightredbooks.net/N5French

DON'T FORGET

Some of the verbs are in the future and conditional tenses. To revise these tenses, refer to page 86.

PART-TIME JOBS – LES PETITS BOULOTS 1

You might already have a part-time job or you might be considering getting one to earn some money. Let's brainstorm some of the jobs you could do. Can you add any others?

Serveur/euse

Vendeur/euse

Baby-sitter

Les petits boulots

Réceptionniste

Caissier/ère

⚙️ ACTIVITY: MY PART-TIME JOB – MON PETIT BOULOT

Read the following sentences and find out where each person works and what jobs they do.

1. Je travaille dans un café, je suis serveur.

2. Je travaille dans un hôtel, je suis réceptionniste.

3. Je travaille dans un magasin, je suis vendeuse/vendeur.

4. Je travaille dans un supermarché, je suis caissier.

5. Je m'occupe des enfants de mes voisins, je suis baby-sitter.

APPLYING FOR A PART-TIME JOB – POSER SA CANDIDATURE POUR UN POSTE

If you are thinking of applying for a part-time job, it would be very useful to put together a CV. Use the links listed to help you write a CV in French. Some of the vocabulary that you will need to write a CV can also be used in the Writing section of your exam. Refer to the chapter on writing (page 84 onwards) to help you.

You may also want to write a cover letter/email in French.

⚙️ ACTIVITY: JOB ADVERTS – LES OFFRES D'EMPLOI

Skim read the following job adverts and try to pick out some key points: what the job is, the hours, the pay and anything else you can understand. Then answer these questions:

1. Which job would you apply for and why?

2. Which job would you not apply for and why?

Advert A

Vous aimez la nourriture? Vous êtes travailleur et motivé? Nous offrons la possibilité de travailler comme serveur/serveuse dans notre petit restaurant familial. Il faut être âgé de plus de 16 ans. Nous proposons un travail de dix heures par semaine. Les repas sont inclus et vous gagnerez sept euros par heure et des pourboires. Vous devez travailler le soir. Veuillez nous contactez au 02 72 54 46 38.

Advert B

Nous proposons un stage professionnel dans un salon de coiffeur. C'est l'occasion idéale d'apprendre les compétences nécessaires pour devenir coiffeur. Vous devez être poli, serviable et enthousiaste. Il faut organiser les rendez-vous des clients, laver les cheveux des clients et travailler à la caisse. Une expérience préalable n'est pas nécessaire. Vous devrez travailler le samedi de neuf heures du matin à cinq heures du soir. Vous gagnerez six euros vingt-cinq de l'heure. Veuillez appeler 01 72 41 25 86.

ONLINE

Head online and check out the links to help you write a CV in French: www.brightredbooks.net/N5French

ONLINE

Look at the links online to help you write a cover letter/email in French: www.brightredbooks.net/N5French

ONLINE

For further practice in reading and working out the meaning of job adverts, refer to the website links in the BrightRED Digital Zone.

contd

Advert C

Vous aimez être en plein air? Nous recherchons des jeunes qui peuvent travailler dans les jardins publics. Vous devez être âgé de 13 à 16 ans et il faut être énergique, honnête et ponctuel. Il faut arroser les plantes et les fleurs. Nous proposons un travail d'une heure après les cours. Vous devez avoir la permission des parents. Vous pourrez travailler près de chez vous et vous gagnerez trente-cinq euros par semaine. Pour plus de renseignements, veuillez appeler 02 72 15 34 67.

 ACTIVITY: WHAT DO YOU DO AT WORK? – QU'EST-CE QUE TU FAIS AU TRAVAIL?

If you already have a part-time job, or for the sake of the Writing exam you are pretending to have a part-time job, you might want to say what your responsibilities and duties are at work.

Read the following phrases and decide which job is being described. Some phrases can be used for more than one job. Don't forget to use your dictionary to look up the meaning of any unfamiliar vocabulary. The jobs being described are:

réceptionniste, caissier/caissière, vendeur/vendeuse, baby-sitter, serveur/serveuse

1. Je dois ranger les vêtements.

2. Il faut servir les clients.

3. Il faut travailler avec le public.

4. Je dois manipuler de l'argent.

5. Je dois m'occuper des enfants et ranger la maison.

6. Je dois vendre des boissons, des magazines et des chips.

7. Il faut classer les documents.

8. Il faut répondre au téléphone.

9. Je dois préparer les sandwichs, le thé et le café.

10. Je dois prendre les réservations.

11. Il faut travailler à l'ordinateur.

12. Je dois aider les enfants avec leurs devoirs.

 ONLINE TEST

Test how well you have learned about part-time jobs at www.brightredbooks.net/N5French.

 ACTIVITY: WHEN DO YOU WORK? – QUAND EST-CE QUE TU TRAVAILLES?

Listen to the people on the audio track talking about when they work and note down:

1. the days that they work
2. the hours they do
3. how much they earn per hour
4. how they get to work.

If you get stuck, read the transcripts below:

A. Je travaille le lundi après-midi et le mercredi soir. Je fais huit heures par semaine et je gagne cinq euros quatre-vingts par heure. Je vais au travail en bus et en train.

B. Je travaille le samedi de neuf heures du matin à cinq heures du soir et le dimanche du midi à quatre heures de l'après-midi. Je fais douze heures par semaine et je gagne six euros trente-cinq de l'heure. Je vais au travail en voiture.

C. Je travaille le jeudi après l'école et le vendredi soir. Je fais six heures par semaine et je gagne sept euros quinze par heure. Je vais au travail à vélo.

D. Je travaille deux fois par semaine: le dimanche matin et le mardi après-midi. Je fais cinq heures par semaine et je gagne six euros quatre-vingt-quinze par heure. Je vais au travail à pied.

THINGS TO DO AND THINK ABOUT

This is a chance for you to revise basic vocabulary such as days of the week, time phrases and numbers. Try drawing a mind map and brainstorming as much vocabulary as possible under these headings:

- days of the week
- months of the year
- time phrases (every month, week, fortnight, sometimes, often, rarely etc.)
- numbers.

PART-TIME JOBS – LES PETITS BOULOTS 2

OPINIONS OF PART-TIME JOBS – LES OPINIONS DES PETITS BOULOTS

Now that you have learned how to say where you work, what job you do, what tasks you do at work, when you work, how much you earn and how you get to work, you should try to give your opinion of your part-time job. It is not enough to say that you like or dislike your job; you must give reasons for your opinions.

You can start with:

- J'adore mon petit boulot car …
- J'aime mon travail parce que …
- Je n'aime pas mon petit boulot car …
- Je déteste mon travail parce que …

Then add the adjective to describe your job (if you don't know the meanings of these adjectives, use your dictionary to look them up):

… c'est …

- intéressant
- génial
- fantastique
- amusant
- facile
- varié
- ennuyeux
- nul
- difficile
- affreux
- fatigant
- bien/mal-payé

 ACTIVITY: OPINIONS – LES OPINIONS

These are very basic opinions and reasons so let's learn some fancier phrases.

Match the French to the English phrases and then decide if the opinion is positive or negative. Try to make links to English words to work out what the phrases mean. If there is still language you don't understand, use your dictionary to look up the meaning.

Les clients sont sympas	My boss is patient and helpful
J'aime travailler en équipe	I have the chance to learn things
Je peux rencontrer de nouvelles personnes	The customers are rude and impatient
Mes collègues sont énervants	I don't have time to study
J'ai beaucoup de choses à faire	Time passes quickly
Je suis très occupé(e)	My colleagues are annoying
Je n'ai pas le temps d'étudier	I like having responsibility
Je peux gagner de l'argent pour financer mes études	I have to wear a uniform and it is not comfortable
Je peux acquérir de l'expérience	The customers are nice
J'aime avoir de la responsabilité	My boss is too strict
J'ai l'occasion d'apprendre des choses	The hours are long
Je ne m'ennuie jamais	I have a lot of things to do
Mon patron est patient et serviable	I can meet new people
Mon patron est trop sévère	I like working in a team
Les clients sont impolis et impatients	I don't have enough free time

contd

Je n'ai pas assez de temps libre	I have to work alone, which is boring
Le temps passe vite	I never get bored
Il faut me lever tôt	I'm very busy
Je dois porter l'uniforme et ce n'est pas confortable	I have to get up early
Les heures sont longues	I can gain experience
Je dois travailler seul, ce qui est ennuyeux	I can earn money to pay for my studies

⚙ ACTIVITY: REVISION – LA RÉVISION

Translate the following paragraphs into English. This is good training for Higher French. If there are sections you are unsure of, try to focus on picking out the main points from the texts. Use a dictionary to look up any unfamiliar vocabulary.

1. Je suis serveuse dans un café au centre-ville. Je dois préparer le thé et le café et servir les clients. Je travaille trois fois par semaine et je gagne cinq euros soixante-dix par heure. J'aime mon travail parce que c'est facile et amusant. Je suis toujours très occupée donc le temps passe vite. En plus, mon patron est patient et mes collègues sont serviables. Je ne m'ennuie jamais, ce qui est génial!

2. Je travaille comme vendeur dans un magasin de vêtements. Je dois aider les clients, ranger le magasin et manipuler de l'argent. Ce que j'aime le plus, c'est que j'ai des réductions et les clients sont polis. Pourtant, parfois, je déteste mon boulot parce que mon patron est trop sévère et impatient. En plus, je dois travailler quatre fois par semaine donc je n'ai pas assez de temps libre. Finalement, mon petit-boulot est mal payé, je ne gagne que cinq euros vingt par heure.

3. Je suis réceptionniste dans un hôtel au bord de la mer. Je dois répondre au téléphone, résoudre les problèmes et prendre les réservations. Je travaille tous les samedis et je fais neuf heures par semaine. C'est bien payé car je gagne sept euros quarante par heure. C'est génial car on me donne des pourboires aussi. Mon patron est très sympa et mes collègues sont gentils.

DON'T FORGET

Refer to the section on describing family members on pages 8–9 if you want to describe your boss or colleagues.

ONLINE TEST

Test how well you have learned about part-time jobs at www.brightredbooks.net/N5French

ONLINE

Have a look at the page about Stanislas and Layla to hear about their part-time jobs and career goals: www.brightredbooks.net/N5French

⚙ ACTIVITY: STUDYING AND WORKING – ÉTUDIER ET TRAVAILLER

If you go to college or university you might decide to find a part-time job to help subsidise your studies. There are advantages and disadvantages of having a part-time job at the same time as studying. Listen to the audio track to hear two people talking about having a part-time job and studying. Can you note down any advantages and disadvantages they mention?

⚠ THINGS TO DO AND THINK ABOUT

Write a paragraph about your part-time job. Even if you don't have a part-time job, pretend that you do! Use the language you have learned in this section to help you. Try to include the following:

- where you work
- what you do
- when you work
- how many hours you work
- how much you earn
- how you get to work
- your opinion of your part-time job
- reasons for your opinion
- any advantages or disadvantages there may be to having a part-time job and studying at the same time.

WORK EXPERIENCE – MON STAGE EN ENTREPRISE

In this section you will learn to describe any work experience you have done. Although you may not have done any work experience yet, you need to be able to write about it in the Writing section of your exam, so use your imagination. This section will also give you the opportunity to revise the perfect and imperfect tenses, which are both used to describe actions completed in the past.

Let's start by thinking of where you might have done your work experience. Can you think of any other examples?

Dans un salon de coiffeur

Dans un magasin

Mon stage en entreprise

Dans un bureau

Dans une école primaire

Dans un restaurant

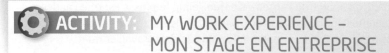

ACTIVITY: MY WORK EXPERIENCE – MON STAGE EN ENTREPRISE

Read the following texts about different people's work experiences. Can you complete the table on page 67?

Try to make links to English to work out what any unfamiliar vocabulary means. Use your dictionary to look up other unfamiliar language.

Marion

J'ai travaillé dans un magasin de sport comme vendeuse. Je commençais à huit heures et demie et je finissais à seize heures. Je devais servir les clients et je travaillais à la caisse. J'ai beaucoup aimé le contact avec le public. Pourtant je n'ai pas aimé le patron car il était désagréable. A mon avis, mon stage était une bonne expérience car c'était varié.

Stéphane

Pendant mon stage en entreprise, j'ai travaillé dans un fast-food. Je commençais à dix heures du matin et je finissais à dix-neuf heures. Je devais préparer les frites et les hamburgers. Ce que j'ai aimé le plus, c'était le travail en équipe. Par contre, j'ai trouvé la journée très longue car à la fin de la journée, j'étais très fatigué. Je pense que mon stage était une mauvaise expérience car c'était monotone.

Laure

J'ai travaillé dans un salon de coiffure. Je commençais à neuf heures et je finissais à dix-huit heures. Pendant mon stage, je devais repondre au téléphone et je devais accuellir les clients. Je préparais le café pour les clients et je rangerais le salon. J'ai aimé le travail car les clients étaient gentils et mon patron était patient et compréhensif. Pourtant, c'était une longue journée et il n'y avait pas beaucoup de pauses pour le personnel. En somme, mon stage était une bonne expérience car c'était facile.

contd

Marcus

Pendant mon stage, j'ai travaillé dans un bureau d'une grande entreprise. Je commençais à neuf heures et je finissais à dix-sept heures trente. Je devais classer les documents et envoyer des emails. J'ai aimé le travail car je m'entendais bien avec mes collègues et j'ai beaucoup appris. En revanche je n'ai pas aimé travailler seul. A mon avis, mon stage était une bonne expérience car c'était intéressant.

	Where did they work?	When did they start?	When did they finish?	What did they do?	What did they like?	What did they not like?	Overall opinion
Marion							
Stéphane							
Laure							
Marcus							

GRAMMAR: THE PERFECT TENSE – LE PASSÉ COMPOSÉ

Look at the reading activity text again. You will notice that each person's work experience is being discussed in the **past tense**. Two tenses are being used, the perfect (*le passé composé*) and the imperfect (*l'imparfait*). To revise the imperfect tense refer to page 47.

This is a great opportunity to revise when the perfect tense is used and how it is formed.

The perfect tense is used to describe a past completed action. It is made up of three parts:

the subject (person/thing doing the verb) + *correct part of avoir/être* (auxiliary verb) + *past participle*

For example: *J'ai joué* – I have played, *Je suis allée* – I have gone

THE PERFECT TENSE WITH AVOIR

1. Let's start with verbs that take avoir in the perfect tense. First, we will revise avoir:

avoir – to have

j'ai	I have	on a	we have
tu as	you have	nous avons	we have
il a	he has	vous avez	you (plural) have
elle a	she has	ils ont –	they have
		elles ont	they have

2. Now add the **past participle**. The past participle is the 'past part' of the verb. In English we usually add 'ed' to the end of the verb to form the past participle, for example played, talked.

   - To form the past participle of an 'er' verb chop off the 'er' and add '<u>é</u>', for example *regarder – regard<u>é</u>*
     J'ai regardé – I have watched

   - To form the past participle of an 'ir' verb chop off the 'ir' and add '<u>i</u>', for example *finir – fin<u>i</u>*
     J'ai fini – I have finished

   - To form the past participle of an 're' verb chop off the 're' and add 'u', for example *vendre – vend<u>u</u>*
     J'ai vendu – I have sold

DON'T FORGET

In your writing, try to use conjunctions, such as *pourtant* and *en somme*, to help structure your writing. Can you think of any more?

ONLINE

For more information about the perfect tense, have a look at the links: www.brightredbooks.net/N5French

ONLINE TEST

Take the test 'Work experience – Mon stage en entreprise' at www.brightredbooks.net/N5French

DON'T FORGET

Let's revise **subject pronouns**:

je	I
tu	you (informal singular)
il	he
elle	she
on	we
nous	we
vous	you (plural/formal)
ils	they
elles	they (feminine)

THINGS TO DO AND THINK ABOUT

Before revising the perfect tense, make sure you know the irregular verbs avoir and être in the present tense.

MORE ON THE PERFECT TENSE – LE PASSÉ COMPOSE – ENCORE!

THE PERFECT TENSE WITH IRREGULAR PAST PARTICIPLES

DON'T FORGET

Avoir is still used as the auxiliary/helping verb with these irregular past participles.

DON'T FORGET

To check the past participle of an irregular verb, use the verb tables in your dictionary.

You have learned how to form regular past participles as these follow a pattern. However, in English we don't always follow the usual pattern of adding 'ed' to the end of the verb: for instance we don't say 'I have doed', we say 'I have done'. In French, just like in English, there are some **irregular past participles** that you will need to learn off by heart. Have a look at this list:

Infinitive	Past participle	Example using 'je'	English meaning
boire – to drink	bu	J'ai bu	I drank/have drunk
lire – to read	lu	J'ai lu	I read/have read
voir – to see	vu	J'ai vu	I saw/have seen
savoir – to know	su	J'ai su	I knew/have known
devoir – to have to	dû	J'ai dû	I had to/have had to
pouvoir – to be able to	pu	J'ai pu	I was able to/have been able to
vouloir – to want to	voulu	J'ai voulu	I wanted to/have wanted to
recevoir – to receive	reçu	J'ai reçu	I received/have received
prendre – to take	pris	J'ai pris	I took/have taken
apprendre – to learn	appris	J'ai appris	I learned/have learned
comprendre – to understand	compris	J'ai compris	I understood/have understood
mettre – to put	mis	J'ai mis	I put/have put
promettre – to promise	promis	J'ai promis	I promised/have promised
conduire – to drive	conduit	J'ai conduit	I drove/have driven
écrire – to write	écrit	J'ai écrit	I wrote/have written
faire – to do/make	fait	J'ai fait	I did/have done
avoir – to have	eu	J'ai eu	I have had/had
être – to be	été	J'ai été	I have been/was

VERBS THAT TAKE ÊTRE IN THE PERFECT TENSE

Some verbs use être as their auxiliary/helping verb instead of avoir. Verbs that take être are usually verbs of motion or indicate a change of state.

The same formula is used: *subject + correct part of être + past participle*

Let's start by revising être:

Etre – to be

je suis	I am
tu es	you are
il est	he is
elle est	she is
on est	we are
nous sommes	we are
vous êtes	you are
ils sont	they are
elles sont	they are

MRS VANDERTRAMP

A good way of remembering verbs that take être is: **MRS VANDERTRAMP**

Infinitive	Past participle	Example using 'je'	English meaning
Monter – to go up	monté	Je suis monté(e)	I went up/have gone up
Rentrer – to go back in	rentré	Je suis rentré(e)	I went back in/have gone back in/returned
Sortir – to go out	sorti	Je suis sorti(e)	I went out/have been out
Venir – to come	venu	Je suis venu(e)	I came/have come
Aller – to go	allé	Je suis allé(e)	I went/have gone
Naître – to be born	né	Je suis né(e)	I was born/have been born
Descendre – to go down	descendu	Je suis descendu(e)	I descended/have gone down
Entrer – to enter	entré	Je suis entré(e)	I entered/have entered
Retourner – to return	retourné	Je suis retourné(e)	I returned/have returned
Tomber – to fall	tombé	Je suis tombé(e)	I fell/have fallen
Rester – to stay	resté	Je suis resté(e)	I stayed/have stayed
Arriver – to arrive	arrivé	Je suis arrivé(e)	I arrived/have arrived
Mourir – to die	mort	Je suis mort(e)	I died/have died
Partir – to leave	parti	Je suis parti(e)	I left/have left

VIDEO LINK

Have a look at the Mrs Vandertramp video at www.brightredbooks.net/N5French

AGREEMENT OF ÊTRE VERBS IN THE PERFECT TENSE

Now let's look at the verb sortir in the perfect tense:

je suis sorti(e)

tu es sorti(e)

il est sorti

elle est sortie

nous sommes sorti(e)s

vous êtes sorti(e)s

ils sont sortis

elles sont sorties

If you look carefully, you will notice that the spelling of *sorti* changes for some of the people. Can you work out why?

When you use être in the perfect tense you must change the past participle depending on the person (it must agree!):

- If the person is feminine, add *e* to the past participle.

- If the person is plural, add an *s* to the past participle.

- If the person is feminine and plural, add *es* to the past participle.

ONLINE

Practise the perfect tense using the link online at www.brightredbooks.net/N5French

ONLINE

For more on this, check out the page on the *passé composé* (www.brightredbooks.net/N5French). Go to the grammar section and start with 'The perfect tense for beginners'.

ONLINE TEST

Take this online test to see how well you can form the perfect tense: www.brightredbooks.net/N5French.

THINGS TO DO AND THINK ABOUT

Now that you have revised the perfect tense, write sentences for each of the following in the perfect tense:

- five avoir verbs with regular past participles

- five avoir verbs with irregular past participles

- five être verbs.

WORK EXPERIENCE ACTIVITIES – LES ACTIVITÉS PENDANT UN STAGE

 ACTIVITY: POSITIVE OR NEGATIVE – POSITIF OU NÉGATIF

Have a look at the following phrases and decide if they are describing something positive or negative about work experience. Put them under the headings *positif* or *négatif*.

1. J'ai dû porter un uniforme, c'était confortable.
2. Il fallait être debout pendant longtemps, c'était fatigant.
3. J'ai passé des heures à travailler à l'ordinateur, c'était monotone.
4. J'ai travaillé dehors, c'était génial.
5. J'ai travaillé avec le public, c'était intéressant.
6. J'ai travaillé en équipe, c'était amusant.
7. J'ai travaillé seul, c'était affreux.
8. J'ai fait l'expérience du commerce, c'était varié.
9. J'ai travaillé dans le domaine du tourisme, c'était fantastique.
10. J'étais responsable de la caisse, je me suis bien amusé(e).
11. Je n'ai rien appris, c'était une perte de temps.
12. J'ai appris à envoyer un fax, c'était utile.

 DON'T FORGET

If there is any language you don't understand, use your dictionary to help you figure out what it means.

ACTIVITY: WHO IS IT? – C'EST QUI?

Listen to the passages about work experience placements on the audio track and answer the questions as best you can. Read the questions first and pick out key words that you think will come up in the text. Listen to the text as many times as you need to in order to answer all the questions.

1. Who worked in a music shop?
2. Who had to wear a uniform?
3. Who learned some new things?
4. Who worked with children?
5. Who went to work by bus?
6. Who met nice people?
7. Who did not work in the evening?
8. Who learned how to operate a till?
9. Who went to work by train?
10. Who worked at the weekend?

⚙ ACTIVITY: REVISION – LA RÉVISION

Read about Lucie's work experience and answer the questions which follow. Look at how many marks each questions is worth and make sure that you write enough information to be awarded full marks.

Lucie

J'ai fait mon stage dans une école primaire. J'y suis allée en bus et à pied. Le voyage a duré trente minutes. Je commençais le travail à neuf heures moins le quart et je finissais à quinze heures dix. J'avais une pause de quinze minutes à dix heures et demie et la pause du déjeuner était à treize heures. J'étais chargée d'aider les enfants à lire dans de petits groupes, d'organiser des jeux et d'aider les élèves à faire leur travail. J'ai aussi aidé les profs à ranger la salle de classe et je devais classer les dossiers des professeurs. J'ai appris à bien communiquer avec les enfants et à organiser des activités. Je me suis bien amusée parce que les enfants étaient vraiment amusants et pleins de vie. À mon avis, mon stage était utile et varié. En effet, j'ai décidé de devenir institutrice à l'avenir.

1. Where did Lucie do her work experience? (1)

2. How did she get to her placement? (2)

3. How long did the journey take? (3)

4. What time did she start work? (1)

5. What time did she finish? (1)

6. When were her breaks? (2)

7. What was she responsible for? (5)

8. What did she learn? (2)

9. Did she enjoy the placement? Why? (4)

10. What has she decided to do as a result of her placement? (1)

VIDEO LINK

Watch the clip 'Qu'est-ce que tu veux faire dans la vie?' to hear about a volunteer work placement and some ideas about what to do in the future: www.brightredbooks.net/N5French

ONLINE TEST

Take the 'Work experience' test online at www.brightredbooks.net/N5French to see how well you know this topic.

THINGS TO DO AND THINK ABOUT

Now it is your turn to write about your work experience using the vocabulary from each of the activities in this section. Refer to the section on writing on page 82 as well to help you.

To be successful in this task, include all information in the bullet points and check the accuracy of your tenses using the previous activities and any other support materials you have. Make sure that your work makes sense: can you translate every word or have you left any words out? Avoid translating directly from English and use your dictionary to check the gender of nouns as well as your spelling and accents.

- Where did you do your work experience?

- How did you get there?

- What time did you start and finish?

- What did you do? Did you learn anything?

- What did you enjoy and why?

- Is there anything you didn't enjoy?

- What is your overall opinion of your work experience?

MY FUTURE PLANS – MES PROJETS POUR L'AVENIR

We touched briefly on future plans when we looked at the qualities and skills needed for different jobs. Now we are going to go into more depth. Can you think of what we could cover in this section?

Prendre une année sabbatique

Continuer mes études

Mes projets pour l'avenir

Gagner de l'argent

Trouver un emploi

Voyager autour du monde

Travailler dans le commerce

DON'T FORGET

There are two future tenses in French (see the last four phrases): the **near future tense** (*futur proche*) states what you *are going to do* and is formed by: subject + aller + infinitive. The simple future tense explains what you *will* do and is formed by: subject + infinitive/future stem + future ending. To revise these tenses refer to page 86.

DON'T FORGET

Je voudrais être professeur means 'I would like to be a teacher'; in French we don't need the indefinite article, the word 'a'.

USEFUL VOCABULARY

Here is some useful vocabulary to start you off. Look up any words you don't understand in the dictionary. You should listen to how these phrases are pronounced on the audio track.

Time phrases:

- plus tard
- à l'avenir

- quand je serai plus grand(e)/âgé(e)
- après le lycée/après la fac

Future plans:

- Je voudrais être pompier.
- Je voudrais travailler comme vétérinaire.
- Je voudrais travailler dans le domaine du commerce.
- J'aimerais devenir infirmier.
- J'aimerais travailler avec les animaux.
- J'ai envie de travailler dans le tourisme.
- J'ai envie de travailler avec les enfants.

- J'ai l'intention de travailler avec le public.
- Je serai coiffeuse.
- J'irai à la fac pour étudier les sciences.
- Je vais faire une formation professionnelle de mécanicien.
- Je vais faire un apprentissage d'électricien.

ACTIVITY: MY IDEAL JOB – MON MÉTIER IDÉAL

Listen to the audio track to hear three people talking about their future plans. Note down as much information as you can about the following:

1. What job do they want to do?

2. Why? (try to name at least four things)

3. What training or qualifications are they going to get?

GRAMMAR

Once you have completed the listening task, read through the transcript online at www.brightredbooks.net/N5French. Is there any vocabulary that you don't know and you need to look up in the dictionary? Have a look at the following phrases taken from the transcript:

contd

- j'aimerais devenir
- j'irai à la fac
- je pourrai rencontrer
- j'aurai l'occasion de

- je gagnerai
- je serai
- je voudrais être
- ce serait génial

Can you remember what the two tenses above are called? Refer to page 86 to revise the conditional, which tells you what someone *would do*, and refer to page 29 to revise the simple future tense, which tells you what someone *will do*.

 ACTIVITY: MY FUTURE PLANS –
MES PROJETS POUR L'AVENIR

Once you have revised these tenses, complete the following sentences, putting the verb in brackets into the simple future tense. Then translate the sentences into English.

1. Je _____ avec le public, peut-être dans un magasin, parce que j'aime le contact avec d'autres personnes. (travailler)

2. Je _____ cuisinier dans un grand restaurant célèbre. (être)

3. J'ai envie de soigner les malades car ça me _____ l'occasion d'aider différentes persons. (donner)

4. Je _____ pour une grande entreprise internationale, peut-être dans le secteur d'informatique. (travailler)

5. Je _____ un métier créatif parce que j'adore le dessin. (faire)

6. Je ne sais pas encore ce que je _____ à l'avenir mais je sais que j'_____ à l'étranger. (faire/habiter)

7. Je _____ un métier qui me _____ de voyager autour du monde. (chercher/permettre)

8. Je _____ un diplôme au lycée technique. (faire)

9. Si je réussis à mes examens, j'_____ à la faculté et je _____ mes études. (aller/continuer)

10. Je _____ joueur de basket professionnel et je _____ beaucoup d'argent. (être/gagner)

 ACTIVITY: WHAT WOULD YOU DO? –
QU'EST-CE QUE TU FERAIS?

Now try the same activity but change the verbs into the conditional tense.

THINGS TO DO AND THINK ABOUT

Now it's your turn. Write about your future plans and do your best to cover the following bullet points. Use the language in this section to help you but personalise the phrases so they are relevant to you. Don't forget that you can learn this and you may wish to use it for your Performance and your writing in the Course assessment.

- What job do you want to do in the future?
- Where would you like to work/live?
- Why do you think you are suitable for this job?
- Why do you want to do this job?
- What training/qualifications do you need to do this job?

 DON'T FORGET

Verbs like *être*, *avoir*, *aller* and *faire* all have irregular stems in the simple future tense and the conditional tense. You can use the verb tables in your dictionary to look them up if you can't remember their irregular forms.

 VIDEO LINK

Check out the clip 'Professions, languages and nationalities' to hear about a variety of jobs you may be interested in: www.brightredbooks.net/N5French

 ONLINE TEST

Take the 'Future plans' test online to see how well you know this topic at www.brightredbooks.net/N5French

CULTURE

HOLIDAYS – LES VACANCES 1

DON'T FORGET

You may also wish to talk about your best holiday/trip as part of your Performance.

VIDEO LINK

The clip 'My favourite holiday' will also give you some extra vocabulary and ideas: www.brightredbooks.net/N5French

REVISION – LA RÉVISION

In this section you will learn how to describe your best holiday/trip and give your opinions on travelling. This section is a great way to revise your past tenses (both perfect and imperfect) – you should refer to pages 43 and 67–9 as well as the vocabulary and phrases you have already learned when revising.

- Où
- Quand
- Avec qui
- Logement
- **Les vacances**
- Activité
- Opinion
- Pendant combien de temps

Let's start by brainstorming all the vocabulary and phrases you know about holidays.

WHEN – QUAND

You could refer to when your holiday is/was in a number of ways:

- en été/en hiver/en automne/au printemps (dernier)
- a Noël
- l'an dernier/l'année dernière
- le mois dernier
- pendant les (grandes) vacances
- il y a un an

WHERE – OÙ

Remember that in French in order to say 'to' or 'in' a country, we use *en* for feminine countries, *au* for masculine countries and *aux* for plural countries. We use *à* for a city or a town.

Here are some examples:

- en France/Espagne/Allemagne
- au Portugal/Maroc/Canada/Pakistan
- aux États-Unis/Pays-Bas
- à Barcelone/Paris/Londres
- à l'étranger
- au bord de la mer/à la campagne/à la montagne
- dans un village/une grande ville

VIDEO LINK

Watch the two 'Holidays in France' clips to hear about where French people go on holiday in July: www.brightredbooks.net/N5French

⚙ ACTIVITY: WITH WHOM – AVEC QUI

You could be going on holiday with a variety of different people. For example:

- avec ma famille/en famille
- avec ma femme
- avec mon ami(e)
- avec mon mari
- avec mes amis
- avec l'école
- tout(e) seul(e)

Remember there are three words for 'my' in French. Try to complete the following grammar rule from memory:

There are three words for 'my' in French. These are _____, _____ and _____. We use ma for _____ words, _____ for masculine words and _____ for plural words.

ACTIVITY: FOR HOW LONG? –
PENDANT COMBIEN DE TEMPS?

You'll need to consider how long your trip lasted:

- quinze jours
- deux semaines
- huit jours/une semaine
- trois mois

Thinking about the length of your trip, try translating the following sentences:

1. En été dernier, je suis allé(e) à Lyon en France pendant quinze jours avec mes amis.
2. Pendant les grandes vacances, je suis parti(e) en famille au bord de la mer en Espagne.
3. A Noël, j'ai passé deux semaines dans un petit village au Canada avec ma mère.
4. Il y a trois ans, je suis allé(e) tout(e) seul(e) à la montagne, en Suisse, pendant un mois.

Now it's your turn – write a sentence about your best holiday/trip.

 ACTIVITY: ACCOMMODATION – LOGEMENT

Choosing from the list below, write in the facilities you could find in the following places.

Logement – accommodation	Equipements/installations – facilities
Dans un hôtel	
Dans une auberge de jeunesse	
Dans un camping	
Dans un gîte	
Chez la famille	
Chez des amis	

une piscine chauffée   un restaurant   un bar   des courts de tennis
une salle de gym   un jardin   un balcon   une belle vue   une grande cuisine
une piste de danse   une salle de jeux   ma propre chambre

Using this vocabulary, write about the accommodation on your holiday. Start with J'ai logé/On a logé ...

 ONLINE TEST

Test yourself on holidays online at www.brightredbooks.net/N5French

 ACTIVITY: LEISURE ACTIVITIES – ACTIVITÉS DE LOISIRS

Here are a few activities you may do on holiday. Check that you understand the meaning of each phrase. You will have many more ideas so just add them to this list.

aller à la plage/piscine
aller en boîte
aller au cinéma
aller au musée
aller au parc d'attraction
faire de la voile
faire de la planche à voile
faire de la natation
faire du sport
faire du ski

faire de l'équitation
lire un roman
écouter de la musique
visiter les environs
manger au restaurant
acheter des souvenirs
se promener
se baigner
bronzer

 THINGS TO DO AND THINK ABOUT

The activities above are in the infinitive to allow you to change them to the imperfect or perfect tense depending on what you want to say. Try writing five sentences about a holiday you have had and what activities you did there.

HOLIDAYS – LES VACANCES 2

VIDEO LINK

Head to the BrightRED Digital Zone and watch the clip 'L'hôtel Guadeloupe', which will give you some extra vocabulary and ideas.

PAST TENSES REMINDER

Remember:

- The perfect tense is an action that is completed in the past, for example *Un jour on est allé au parc d'attraction.*

- The imperfect tense is used for regular actions in the past/interrupted actions and descriptions, for example *Tous les soirs on allait au restaurant pour y déguster les spécialités de la région.*

- You can, however, leave verbs in the infinitive, for example *Je passais mes journées à + infinitive.*

ADDING INTEREST

To make this section more interesting and not just one long list of activities, you may wish to use the following expressions:

- On passait nos journées à + infinitive

- Quand il pleuvait on/je (+ imperfect) ...

- Quand il faisait beau on/je (+ imperfect) ...

- Tous les jours on/je (+ imperfect) ...

- Un jour on/je (+ perfect) ...

- Une fois on/je (+ perfect) ...

 ACTIVITY: GRAMMAR/TRANSLATION ACTIVITY – UNE EXERCISE DE GRAMMAIRE/TRADUCTION

Look at the following three paragraphs. Fill in the gaps by translating the verb into French and deciding whether you will use it in the perfect or imperfect tense or leave it in the infinitive. You can then try to translate the three paragraphs.

Veronique

1. L'année dernière en hiver je _____ (*to go*) en France avec mes parents. On _____ (*to spend*) nos journées à _____ (*to ski*) dans les Alpes et puis le soir on _____ (*to go*) au restaurant pour _____(*to eat*) de bons repas chauds. Un jour on _____ (*to go*) dans la ville la plus proche pour _____ (*to buy*) quelques souvenirs pour la famille et les amis.

Olivier

2. Il y a trois ans je _____ (*to leave*) en Espagne avec mes amis. Tous les jours on _____ (*to go*) à la plage ou on _____ (*to stay*) au bord de la piscine pour _____ (*to sunbathe*). On _____ (*to spend*) nos soirées en boite de nuit parce qu'on _____ _____ (*to love to dance*). Un jour on _____ (*to windsurf*).

Rose

3. Pendant les grandes vacances je _____ (*to go*) en Italie avec ma mère. Les jours de soleil on _____ (*to walk*) dans de petits villages, on _____ (*to visit*) les environs ou on _____ (*to drink*) un verre à la terrasse des cafés. Un jour on _____ (*to go*) à Rome pour _____ (*to visit*) les attractions touristiques et pour _____ (*to go shopping*).

VIDEO LINK

Check out the 'Travelling to France' clip at www.brightredbooks.net/N5French for the first instalment of Michael's video diary about planning a holiday in France.

ACTIVITY: OPINION OF THE TRIP – OPINION SUR LE VOYAGE

You will always have an opinion of your trip. Decide if the following expressions are positive or negative and put them under the heading *positive* or *negative*.

C'était super   Le personnel était très serviable   Je me suis bien amusé(e)

C'était intéressant   Je n'y retournerai pas   Les gens étaient très impolis

C'était amusant   Il pleuvait tous les jours   C'était ennuyeux

Je recommanderais ce genre de voyage   Il n'y avait rien à faire

Les gens étaient très accueillants   Les gens n'étaient pas gentils

La nourriture était délicieuse   C'était nul!   C'était sale

La nourriture n'était pas très bonne   Les gens étaient très aimables

ACTIVITY: THE IMPORTANCE OF TRAVEL – L'IMPORTANCE DE VOYAGER

You could also add why you think travel is important.

In groups try to think, in French, of ways of saying you like to travel and reasons why.

Listen to the audio track and match the parts of the sentences:

Saying you love to travel	Reasons
J'adore voyager parce que/car ...	... on découvre de nouvelles cultures et traditions.
J'aime aller à l'étranger parce que/car ...	... voir comment vivent d'autres personnes.
J'aime partir en vacances parce que/car ...	... on se fait de nouveaux amis.
J'aime visiter des pays étrangers parce que/car ...	... de découvrir d'autres pays et d'apprendre une autre langue.
Il est important de voyager pour ...	... on se détend et on oublie la vie quotidienne.
A mon avis voyager est un bon moyen ...	... on profite du beau temps.

Now try to translate them into English.

VIDEO LINK

Watch the 'Staying in a castle' clip at www.brightredbooks.net/N5French for more vocabulary.

ACTIVITY: CÉDRIC'S BEST HOLIDAY – LES MEILLEURES VACANCES DE CÉDRIC

Before you try to write about your best holiday, listen to Cédric talking about his best holiday. Complete the table by putting in as much information as you can.

Quand – when	
Où – where	
Avec qui – with whom	
Pendant combien de temps – for how long	
Logement – accommodation	
Activité – activities	
Opinion – opinion	

DON'T FORGET

When writing about a past event make sure you:
• use the perfect and imperfect correctly
• agree the past participles for feminine and plural
• add some opinions
• always check your written accuracy.

ONLINE TEST

Test yourself on holidays online at www.brightredbooks.net/N5French.

THINGS TO DO AND THINK ABOUT

Now it's your turn. Using all the phrases and passages above to help you, write about a past holiday you have been on.

EVENTS, LITERATURE AND FILM – LES TRADITIONS, LA LITERATURE ET LES FILMS

CELEBRATING A SPECIAL EVENT – CÉLÉBRATION D'UN ÉVÉNEMENT SPÉCIAL

As part of the National 5 course you will be discovering new things about different traditions, special events and cultures in the countries in which French is spoken. It would be impossible to cover every eventuality in this book.

This may be the perfect opportunity for you to do some individual research on an aspect of the culture of a Francophone country. You could present your findings as part of your Performance.

Here are some traditions and cultural events that you may wish to find out more about:

ACTIVITY: TRADITIONS AND SPECIAL EVENTS – LES TRADITIONS ET ÉVENEMENTS SEPCIAUX

Here is some vocabulary you may wish to use when talking about traditions and special events. Try to work out what the words mean in English.

Verb	English
fêter	
manger	
boire	
danser	
chanter	
se déguiser	
prier	

Noun	English
une fête	
des cadeaux	
un gâteau	
les feux d'artifices	
du champagne	
un déguisement	

Use the words above to describe a special event or tradition in Scotland.

LITERATURE AND FILM – LA LITERATURE ET LES FILMS

In this section you will learn how to talk about any books you have read or films you have seen. The language used to describe books and films is very similar so we will look at both together.

Let's start by thinking about what you might like to say about a book or a film:

- What is the book/film about?
- Who are your favourite characters/actors?
- What is your opinion of the book/film?

ACTIVITY: WHAT IS THE BOOK/FILM ABOUT? – DE QUOI PARLE LE FILM/LE LIVRE?

Read the sentences/phrases below and translate them into English. You may wish to change or complete them to talk about a book you have just read or a film you have seen.

Le livre/le film se passe au 20ième siècle et a lieu dans le sud de la France.

Le livre/le film parle de ...

Le livre/le film raconte l'histoire de ...

ONLINE TEST

Test yourself on events, literature and film online at www.brightredbooks.net/ N5French

ACTIVITY: YOUR FAVOURITE CHARACTERS – TES PERSONAGES PRÉFÉRÉS

Here are some adjectives which can be used to describe characters (refer back to pages 8–9 in the Family and friends section for more examples).

Write out the feminine versions and English translations of these adjectives. Then use some of the adjectives to describe your favourite characters/actors.

Masculine	Feminine	English
beau		
marrant		
méchant		
crédible		
ennuyeux		
jeune		
vieux		

Mon personnage/acteur préféré était/est _____ car il/elle est + *adjective*

Je trouve les personnages/acteurs très crédibles ce qui rend le livre/le film plus intéressant.

Les personnages du livre/du film sont/étaient intéressants car ...

Selon moi/à mon avis/je trouve que le scénario est très intéressant et j'ai bien aimé la relation entre les personnages.

ACTIVITY: YOUR OPINIONS – TES OPINIONS

Look at these opinions about a book/film and decide if they are positive or negative, then translate them into English.

Ce que j'ai vraiment aimé c'est ...

J'ai vraiment aimé le livre/le film car ...

Je trouvais le film un peu long mais j'ai vraiment aimé les acteurs et l'histoire.

Je n'avais jamais lu/vu ce genre de livre/de film mais je le recommanderais car l'histoire est vraiment intéressante.

Je n'ai pas aimé ce livre/ce film car l'histoire était très ennuyeuse.

J'ai été déçu par la fin du livre/du film.

J'ai beaucoup appris/découvert sur la culture française par exemple, les français attachent beaucoup d'importance à passer du temps en famille autour d'un bon repas.

Normalement, je ne regarde jamais les films scientifiques/d'amour/d'action mais ce film m'a beaucoup plu.

J'ai vraiment aimé ce film et je regarderai bien d'autres films de ce genre à l'avenir.

Je recommanderais ce livre/ce film parce que l'histoire m'a beaucoup intéressée et j'aime beaucoup les acteurs.

Je ne recommanderais pas ce livre/ce film car il n'était pas intéressant et il ne se passe rien.

Je n'ai pas aimé ce film car je n'aime pas les films d'action trop violents.

THINGS TO DO AND THINK ABOUT

Take some of the sentences from the activities above and write a short paragraph about your favourite book/film.

EVENTS, LITERATURE AND FILM – LES TRADITIONS, LA LITERATURE ET LES FILMS

DON'T FORGET

Top tips:
- Read each question.
- Try to find the answers in the text using the questions to help you.
- Only use your dictionary if absolutely necessary.

VIDEO LINK

You may also wish to watch the BBC clip 'My favourite films and directors' at www.brightredbooks.net/N5French to enhance your vocabulary.

ACTIVITY: OPINIONS ON A FILM – AVIS SUR UN FILM

Read the following text, in which Yannick describes a film he has just seen. Answer the questions that follow.

Yannick donne son avis d'un film qu'il vient de voir

La semaine dernière, je suis allé au cinéma pour voir un film britannique. Le film était en anglais et a lieu dans un petit village dans le sud de l'Angleterre. Le film raconte l'histoire de quatre amis qui ne se sont pas vus depuis 15 ans et qui se retrouvent pour un week-end dans une petite maison. Au début les personnages s'entendent très bien et se rappellent de bons moments de leur jeunesse. Mais au cours du film, il commence à y avoir de la tension entre eux. A la fin du film ils se rendent compte que leur vie a changé et qu'ils n'ont plus rien en commun. Mon personnage préféré est Louisa, car elle est très bonne actrice et très crédible dans le rôle.

Le film était assez intéressant et les acteurs jouaient bien. C'était bien de voir un film sous-titré pour pouvoir améliorer mon anglais.

1. When did Yannick see the film? (1)

2. Where does the film take place? (1)

3. What is the film about? (1)

4. What happens:
   at the beginning of the film? (1)
   during the film? (1)
   at the end of the film? (2)

5. Why is Louisa Yannick's favourite character? Mention **two** things. (2)

6. What is Yannick's overall impression of the film? Tick the correct box. (1)

Yannick thought the film was uninteresting and boring.	
Yannick thinks French films are better and the actors were good.	
Yannick likes watching films with subtitles as they help to improve his English.	

Now it's your turn. Write about a film you have seen using the vocabulary and expressions you have learned. Again you may wish to use some of this for your performance.

ACTIVITY: SYLVIE'S OPINIONS ON A BOOK – LES AVIS DE SYLVIE SUR UN LIVRE

Now listen to Sylvie talking about a book she has just read. Complete the text below by choosing the correct word from the box for each gap.

Sylvie parle d'un livre qu'elle vient de lire

Je viens de lire un livre très (1)_____. Le livre a lieu en (2)_____ et c'est une histoire vraie qui raconte l'expérience un couple de (3)_____ britannique qui déménage dans un petit village en France. Au (4)_____ ils trouvent la vie un peu difficile car ils ne (5)_____ pas la langue et la grande ville leur manque. Mais au bout de quelques (6)_____ ils font la connaissance de villageois et (7)_____ à mieux parler français. Mon personnage (8)_____ est Paul, l'homme du couple. Il est très (9)_____ et optimiste que tout allait bien se passer. A la fin du livre il adore vivre dans ce petit village et il apprécie (10)_____ la culture et la bonne cuisine (11)_____. J'ai vraiment aimé ce livre et je le recommanderais car il est à la fois émouvant et (12)_____.

1. intéressant/intéressante	2. 2004/2005
3. retraités/retraitées	4. debout/début
5. parlent/parle	6. moi/mois
7. commence/commencent	8. préféré/préférée
9. marrante/marrant	10. beacoup/beaucoup
11. français/française	12. drôle/drôlée

 ONLINE TEST

Test yourself on events, literature and film online at www.brightredbooks.net/N5French.

THINGS TO DO AND THINK ABOUT

Now you have all the vocabulary and phrases you need to describe literature and film, you may wish to start reading and/or watching films in French. This is great way to improve your language skills and also gives you an insight into the culture of Francophone countries.

Write about a book you have read using the vocabulary and expressions you have learned. You may wish to use some of this for your Performance.

COURSE ASSESSMENT: WRITING

INTRODUCTION AND BULLET POINT 1

The aim of this section is to ensure you feel fully prepared for the Writing section of the Course assessment.

You will be revising some of the vocabulary and grammatical structures you have already visited in this book and will build on these to allow you to produce an accurate piece of writing that you feel comfortable with and are able to reproduce and adapt slightly on the day of your Course assessment.

The writing part of the Course assessment is worth a total of 20 marks and will be 120–150 words in length. You may wish to write more, but remember that accuracy is key.

So let's begin!

WHAT IS EXPECTED?

First of all, let's look at what you will be expected to write.

You will be expected to write an email in response to a job advert. The job advert will be in French, advertising the job and giving other relevant details, such as the type of person you must be and whom to contact.

You will then have to write your email based on the four predictable bullet points (these will always be the same) and the two less predictable bullet points (these will change from year to year, but will always be in the context of applying for the job).

Below is an example of the job advert and the bullet points you will to have to address. The first four bullet points are the predictable ones and the remaining two the less predictable ones.

You are preparing an application for the job advertised below and you write an email in French to the company.

Café Georges au centre de Bruxelles cherche **serveur/serveuse**.

Vous devez être motivé et dynamique et savoir parler le français et l'anglais.

Pour plus de détails ou si ce poste vous intéresse contactez Mme Georges à l'adresse suivante cafegeorges@fsnet.fr.com.

Veuillez joindre votre CV et répondre par email, incluant les détails suivants.

To help you to write your email, you have been given the following checklist of information to give about yourself. You must deal with all of these points:

- personal details (name, age, where you live)
- school/college education experience until now
- skills/interests you have which make you right for the job
- related work experience
- when you will be available for interview and to work
- any links to Belgium or another French-speaking country.

Use all of the above to help you write the email in French, which should be 120–150 words. You may use a French dictionary.

As you will be talking about yourself in this email it is important to go back and revise present tense verbs, especially the **big four** (avoir, etre, aller, faire) and endings (refer to page 7).

We will take each bullet point in turn.

BULLET POINT 1: PERSONAL DETAILS (NAME, AGE, WHERE YOU LIVE)

This should be a very straightforward start as you will have seen and used these phrases in many other contexts. However you must know how to *spell* these sentences.

Test yourself: Choose the correct phrase from the following.

Name

Je m'applle …	Je ma pelle …	Je m'appelle …
Mon famille nom est …	Mon nom de famille est …	Mon surnom est …

Age

Je suis 16 ans	J'ai 16	J'ai 16 ans
Mon anniversaire est le 12 mai	Mon anniversary le 26 octobre	Mon anniversaire est le 4th juin

Where you live

J'habeet …	J'habite …	Je habite …
à Ayr en Eccosse	à Glagow a Ecossais	à Inverness en Ecosse

How did you do? It is really important that you get off to a good start and ensure your basic French is accurate.

This first bullet point does not allow for a lot of extra French, although you may wish to write more about where you live. (Refer back to the section on town compared to country in the Society chapter (pages 40–1) for a recap of relevant vocabulary.)

Look at the following examples and translate them into English.

Some words have been underlined so that you can adapt the passage to suit your needs.

> **EXAMPLE**
>
> Bonjour, je m'appelle <u>Thomas</u> et j'ai <u>16</u> ans. Mon anniversaire est le <u>16 octobre</u> et j'aurai <u>17</u> ans. J'habite à <u>Thurso</u> dans le <u>nord-est</u> de l'Ecosse. <u>Thurso</u> est une <u>petite ville</u> <u>au bord de la mer</u> et il y a environ <u>10 000</u> habitants.

> **EXAMPLE**
>
> Je m'appelle <u>Julie</u> et mon nom de famille est <u>Brown</u>. J'ai <u>15</u> ans mais j'aurai <u>16</u> ans dans <u>deux semaines</u>. J'habite dans un <u>petit village à la campagne</u> qui se trouve à <u>20 minutes de Glasgow et à 30 minutes d'Edimbourg</u>, qui est la capitale de l'Ecosse.

> **EXAMPLE**
>
> Bonjour, je m'appelle <u>Christina</u> et j'aurai <u>19</u> ans le <u>12 septembre</u>. En ce moment j'habite à <u>Perth</u> qui se trouve <u>au centre</u> de l'Ecosse mais je suis d'origine <u>polonaise</u>. J'habite en Ecosse depuis <u>10 ans</u> et j'aime bien ce pays car le paysage est magnifique.

> **EXAMPLE**
>
> Je m'appelle <u>John Mackay</u> et j'ai <u>17</u> ans. Je vis à <u>Glasgow</u> en Ecosse dans un quartier qui s'appelle <u>Mosspark</u>. J'aime bien mon quartier car il y a beaucoup à faire et tous mes amis y habitent.

DON'T FORGET

If you are struggling with some of the words, speak to your teacher/lecturer to see if you could make any changes.

VIDEO LINK

Watch the clip 'J'habite à Dijon' at www.brightredbooks.net/N5French

VIDEO LINK

Watch the clip 'How to introduce yourself' at www.brightredbooks.net/N5French

ONLINE TEST

Take the 'Writing: Introduction and personal details' test online at www.brightredbooks.net/N5French

Top tips

- Always write sentences that *you* feel comfortable with and that you can cope with when you have to write them off by heart.
- Start learning each paragraph as you write it so you can reproduce it accurately on the day.
- Read your paragraph.
- Cover the first sentence and try to write it out.
- Check.
- Repeat the process until you have written the whole paragraph accurately.

THINGS TO DO AND THINK ABOUT

Now it's your turn. Write a short paragraph on the first bullet point, including:

- your name
- your age
- where you live.

BULLET POINT 2: SCHOOL/COLLEGE EDUCATION EXPERIENCE UNTIL NOW 1

WHAT TO INCLUDE

This bullet point is about your education experience until now. Let us think about what you may wish to include. If you have already studied the Learning context, then you will already be familiar with a lot of the vocabulary and grammatical structures required to complete this bullet point.

Looking at the spider diagram, it makes sense to start with a brief description of the school/college you are attending.

USEFUL PHRASES

Here are some possible phrases you could use:

Je suis élève à …

Cette année, je suis en première et j'apprends six matières.

Je fréquente _____ où je suis en train de préparer mes examens qui auront lieu au mois de mai.

Puisque j'ai des examens cette année je passe tout mon temps à étudier.

Quant à mon école, c'est une grande école/un grand lycée/une petite école/un petit lycée avec environ 800/500 élèves et 80/40 profs.

J'aime bien mon école/lycée parce que les profs sont, en général, très sympas et j'y ai beaucoup d'amis.

VOCABULARY FOR WHICH SUBJECTS YOU STUDIED

Looking at the spider diagram, four of the points mention your subjects, so it is *really* important that you know these and their gender.

Les matières

Les langues étrangères
le français	l'allemand	l'espagnol	l'italien	
l'urdu	le gaélique	le polonais	le russe	le chinois

Les sciences
la physique	la chimie	la biologie

Les matières obligatoires
l'anglais	les maths

D'autres matières
l'histoire	la géographie	les études modernes/la politique	
le dessin	les arts dramatiques	l'EPS/le sport	la musique

SUBJECTS STUDIED LAST YEAR/SUBJECTS BEING STUDIED NOW

To avoid boring the marker and making too many mistakes, try not to list all the subjects you did last year and all the subjects you are doing this year. Here are some ways you could avoid this:

L'année dernière j'ai fait 6 matières y compris + *two subjects* (*do not forget the article*). Cette année j'ai décidé d'étudier + *subjects* (*do not forget the article*) au niveau National 4/National 5/Higher.

L'an dernier j'ai étudié 8 matières y compris + *three subjects* (*do not forget the article*) mais cette année je n'étudie que + *subjects.* (*do not forget the article*)

L'année dernière j'ai étudié 6 matières y compris + *two subjects* (*do not forget the article*). Cette année je fais + (du/de la/de l'/des) *subjects* au niveau National 4/National 5/Higher.

When using *faire* with subjects you must change the **definite article**, that is *le/la/l'/les*, to the partitive, that is *du/de la/de l'/des*.

SUBJECTS YOU LIKED/DIDN'T LIKE AND WHY/WHY NOT

Again this should already be quite familiar to you, but it is always good to recap so here are some expressions you could use to give your opinions and talk about subjects you like/dislike:

Opinions

Je trouve que ...   Je pense que ...   A mon avis ...   Selon moi ...

Subjects you like/dislike

Love/like	**Dislike/hate**
J'adore ...	Je déteste ...
J'aime ...	Je n'aime pas ...
Ma matière préférée est ...	La matière dont j'ai horreur ...
Mes matières préférées sont ...	La matière que j'aime le moins ...

VIDEO LINK

Check out the 'Les cours et les devoirs' clip at www.brightredbooks.net/N5French.

 THINGS TO DO AND THINK ABOUT

Let's look more closely at what we could say about the subjects we like/dislike.

Put the phrases below under the headings *positif* or *négatif*.

Je suis fort(e) en ...   Je suis faible en ...
A mon avis _____ est très utile.   Je trouve _____ très facile.

Je reçois toujours de bonnes notes en ...
Selon moi _____ est trop difficile.

Je reçois toujours de mauvaises notes en ...
J'ai décidé d'étudier _____ car j'en ai besoin pour ma future carrière.

Je pense que le prof est marrant et il ne nous donne pas trop de devoirs.
A mon avis il est très important d'étudier _____ car _____.
Je trouve que le prof est trop strict et il ne nous aide pas quand on a des difficultés.
J'ai choisi _____ parce que c'est une matière qui m'intéresse.

A mon avis _____ est une perte de temps.

BULLET POINT 2: SCHOOL/COLLEGE EDUCATION EXPERIENCE UNTIL NOW 2

VIDEO LINK

Watch the clip 'Qu'est-ce que tu veux faire dans la vie?' at www.brightredbooks.net/N5French

FUTURE ASPIRATIONS

The second bullet point is probably the best place to add what you would like to do in the future.

Quick reminder

To say what you will do or would like to do later on in life, you will have to use the future or conditional tense. Here is a quick reminder:

Future	Conditional
Take the infinitive	Take the infinitive
Add endings	Add endings
ai, as, a, ons, ez, ont (similar to avoir)	*ais, ais, ait, ions, iez, aient* (like imperfect)
Exceptions	*Exceptions*
être – serai	être – serais
avoir –aurai	avoir –aurais
aller – irai	aller – irais
faire – ferai	faire – ferai

DON'T FORGET

Remember there is no article for jobs.

Other exceptions include pouvoir, savoir, devoir and vouloir.

Now let's look at how you can add what you would like to do in the future. It may be worth linking this to the job and/or languages.

Quand je quitterai l'école j'aimerais aller à la fac pour étudier ...

A l'avenir j'aimerais être ...

Après avoir fini mes études, j'aimerais prendre une année sabbatique et travailler à l'étranger/en France.

Quand je quitterai l'université j'aimerais passer un an au Québec pour améliorer mon français.

Je ne sais pas encore ce que je veux faire après l'école mais un jour j'aimerais vivre à l'étranger.

ONLINE TEST

Take the 'School/college education experience until now' test online at www.brightredbooks.net/N5French.

THINGS TO DO AND THINK ABOUT

You are now ready and armed with all the phrases you need to write your second bullet point. To help you a little more and also to give you some listening practice, try to complete the following passages about school using the words given in the box below. For a bigger challenge, try not to look at the words.

1. En ce moment, je suis en première au Lycée Ampère. Mon école est très _____ et moderne et il y a environ _____ profs et 1000 élèves. J'aime assez bien mon école car j'y ai beaucoup d'_____ et en général je m'_____ très bien avec tous mes profs.

   L'année _____ j'ai fait 8 matières y compris l'anglais, les maths et l'_____. Cette année j'_____ le français, l'_____, l'espagnol et le dessin. J'adore les langues _____ car selon moi il est très important de _____ parler au moins deux langues de nos _____. Par contre, je n'aime pas trop le dessin. Je _____ que le prof est très _____ et nous donne trop de _____.

   Quand je _____ l'école, j'aimerais aller à la fac pour étudier le _____ et l'espagnol. A l'avenir j'aimerais _____ et vivre à l'_____.

entends	amis	allemand	savoir	sévère
cent	dernière	étranger	jours	français
grande	étudie	étrangères	trouve	devoirs
quitterai	travailler	anglais		

2. Je suis _____ au Lycée Jean Macé ou je suis en _____ de préparer mes examens. Mon lycée est assez _____ mais il est très _____. J'ai de bons rapports avec tous mes profs car ils sont _____ prêts à aider.

   L'an _____ j'ai étudié 9 matières y compris, les maths, les sciences et la _____. Cette _____ je fais du français, des maths, de l'anglais, des sciences et de l'_____. Ma matière préférée, c'est les maths. Je trouve cette _____ très facile et je suis très _____ en maths. D'ailleurs j'ai toujours de bonnes _____. Par _____ la matière dont j'ai horreur c'est la biologie. Je trouve ça trop _____ et à mon _____ c'est inutile.

   A l'_____ j'aimerais aller à la fac pour faire des études de _____. Un jour je veux avoir mon _____ cabinet et bien sûr gagner beaucoup d'_____.

train	avenir	élève	matière	dernier
droit	grand	musique	difficile	vieux
notes	histoire	toujours	propre	forte
contre	avis	argent	année	

BULLET POINT 3: SKILLS/INTERESTS YOU HAVE WHICH MAKE YOU RIGHT FOR THE JOB

This bullet point allows you to write about any skills and/or interests you may have which make you the ideal candidate.

VIDEO LINK
Check out the 'Talking about your work' clip at www.brightredbooks.net/N5French

POSSIBLE WAYS OF STARTING

1. Je veux poser ma candidature pour ce poste parce que …
2. Je suis la personne idéale pour ce poste parce que …
3. Je serais le candidat idéal/la candidate idéale parce que …

These phrases could be followed with a number of different adjectives and phrases. Look at the examples below and choose the ones you feel most comfortable with to complete your sentence.

Je suis …

- travailleur(se)
- gentil(le)
- créatif(ve)
- très ponctuel(le)
- toujours poli(e) et aimable
- toujours souriant(e)
- enthousiaste
- sérieux(se)

Personal qualities

- Je parle couramment le français et l'allemand.
- Je crois que je suis quelqu'un à qui on peut faire confiance.
- On peut toujours compter sur moi.

Refer to page 63 for more phrases about qualities for different jobs.

Other reasons

- J'aimerais gagner de l'expérience en travaillant et en vivant à l'étranger.
- J'adore visiter d'autres pays et faire la connaissance de nouvelles personnes.
- J'aimerais améliorer mon français et découvrir une nouvelle culture.
- J'adore les langues vivantes et j'aimerais me perfectionner en français.
- J'apprends le français depuis 5 ans et j'aimerais travailler en France pour perfectionner mon français.

VIDEO LINK
Watch the clip 'Talking about the working day' at www.brightredbooks.net/N5French

SKILLS PHRASES FOR SPECIFIC JOBS

The phrases above are very general and could be used for any job. Below are some more phrases that are suited to specific jobs.

Tourisme

- Je suis attiré(e) par une carrière dans le tourisme.
- J'aime travailler en équipe.
- Je m'entends très bien avec tout le monde.
- J'aime le contact avec les gens/les clients.

Musée

- Je m'intéresse à l'art/à la peinture/à l'histoire.

Animateur/travail avec les enfants

- Je m'entends très bien avec les enfants.
- J'adore les enfants et je fais du babysitting régulièrement.

contd

- J'ai beaucoup d'énergie et d'enthousiasme.

Vignes/ferme/camping

- J'aimerais travailler dehors/en plein air.

- Plus tard quand je quitterai l'école j'aimerais travailler avec les enfants.

- J'aime les animaux.

VIDEO LINK

Have a look at the clip 'Working in a ski resort' at www.brightredbooks.net/N5French.

INTERESTS RELEVANT TO THE JOB

This bullet point also asks you to mention any interests you may have that may make you right for the job. Really think about this: watching TV or spending time talking to your friends on Facebook etc. are probably not the interests most employers are looking for.

Again, as with bullet point 1, you will have a lot of phrases to talk about your interests. Here are just some ideas of how to make your sentences more interesting.

DON'T FORGET

There will be many other phrases you may wish to use, but just remember you are applying for a job so keep it concise and relevant.

Possible ways of introducing interests

- Pendant mon temps libre j'aime ...
- Quand j'ai du temps libre j'aime ...
- Pour me détendre je passe mon temps libre à + *infinitive*.
- Je m'intéresse à la/au/à l'/aux ...

- Je me passionne pour ...
- J'aime bien ...
- Mon passe-temps préféré est _____ car ...

VIDEO LINK

For more about the qualities necessary for work watch the video 'The world of work' at www.brightredbooks.net/N5French

Sports

- Je suis très sportif(ve) et je fais du jogging tous les jours. A mon avis il est très important de faire de l'exercice physique pour rester en forme.
- Je fais partie d'un club de ...

- Le sport joue un rôle très important dans ma vie.
- Quand il fait beau j'adore faire des randonnées à vélo ou me promener.

ONLINE TEST

Take the 'Skills/interests you have which make you right for the job' test online at www.brightredbooks.net/N5French.

Musique

- Pour me reposer je passe mon temps à écouter de la musique.
- Je me détends en écoutant de la musique.

- Je joue de la guitare/du piano depuis cinq ans.
- Je suis passionné(e) par la musique.

DON'T FORGET

You can revise more hobbies by flicking to the section 'loisirs' (pp 22–5).

Autres intérêts

- J'adore le cinéma et surtout les films étrangers.
- Je m'intéresse beaucoup à l'histoire et donc je vais souvent aux musées.
- Je suis très doué(e) en dessin et j'aime beaucoup peindre et dessiner quand j'ai du temps libre.

- J'adore lire et donc la lecture joue un rôle très important dans ma vie.
- Puisque j'ai des examens cette année je passe la plupart de mon temps à faire mes devoirs.

THINGS TO DO AND THINK ABOUT

A bit of a challenge now: try to translate the following sentences into French. This is a really difficult skill but use the phrases you have just learned to help you.

1. I would like to apply for the job as I would like to improve my French.
2. I love travelling and this job would allow me to discover a new culture.
3. I am very hard working and I love working in a team.
4. I would be the ideal person for this job as I am polite and I get on very well with everyone.
5. When I leave school I would like to travel and work abroad.
6. In my free-time I love doing sport. I am in a hockey club and I train every weekend.
7. When I have time I love to go for long walks with my dogs. This keeps me fit and I like being in the fresh air.
8. I am very interested in music and at the moment I am learning how to play the flute.
9. I am very passionate about art and I love to spend my time visiting art galleries.
10. When the weather is nice I like to go horse-riding in the countryside.

BULLET POINT 4: RELATED WORK EXPERIENCE

In this section you will be required to write about any related work experience you may have. This could be about your work experience week or a full-time/part-time job you may currently have. Refer to pages 66–7 to revise the topic of work experience.

QUICK REMINDER

Let's start with any work experience you may have done. You will need to use the perfect and imperfect tenses, so here's just a quick reminder. Refer back to pages 43 and 67–9 if you need more practice on these tenses.

Perfect tense

1. Present tense of avoir or être.

2. Past participle – take the infinitive and remove 'er', 'ir' or 're' and add 'é' to 'er' verbs, 'i' to 'ir' verbs and 'u' to 're' verbs.

3. Remember to learn the irregular verbs, especially the big four: avoir, être, aller and faire.

Imperfect tense

1. Take the present tense 'nous' form of any verb, remove the 'ons' and add the following endings: ais, ais, ait, ions, iez, aient.

2. Great news: the only exception is être.

DON'T FORGET ➕

As the only exception in the imperfect tense is être, you should know it by heart!

PAST WORK EXPERIENCE

Now we can start to write about past work experience.

Time phrases

- L'année dernière
- Il y a un an
- Pendant les grandes vacances

Where you worked

J'ai fait un stage/J'ai travaillé ...

- dans un restaurant
- dans un supermarché
- dans un bureau
- dans un magasin de vêtements
- dans une bibliothèque
- dans une école primaire

or

DON'T FORGET ➕

You can refer back to the employability section for more jobs.

- J'ai travaillé comme + job (remember no article before the job)

| serveur(se) | assistant(e) | femme de chambre |
| cassier(ère) | vendeur(e) | |

ACTIVITY: WHAT YOU DID – CE QUE VOUS AVEZ FAIT

Match the French phrases to the English.

Je devais ...

mettre les tables	look after the children
débarrasser les tables	play with children
classer les dossiers	set the tables
servir les clients	welcome customers
m'occuper des enfants	clear the tables
répondre au téléphone	sort out the files
jouer avec les enfants	serve customers
prendre des commandes	answer the phone
accueillir les clients	take orders

What you thought of it

As you are applying for a job you may wish to make this a positive experience. Here are a few examples of some opinions you could give.

J'ai vraiment aimé ce stage car/parce que ...

- ça m'a donné une première expérience du monde du travail
- j'ai beaucoup appris
- je me suis fait(e) de nouveaux amis en dehors du collège/lycée
- je me suis bien entendu(e) avec tous mes collègues
- c'était intéressant
- j'ai pu gagner mon propre argent

You can mix and match the reasons above, but remember to use the ones you feel most comfortable with and will be able to remember and reproduce accurately.

 VIDEO LINK

Check out the clip 'Qu'est-ce que tu veux faire dans la vie?' at www.brightredbooks.net/N5French

 ACTIVITY: YANNICK'S WORK EXPERIENCE

Listen to the audio track and answer the following questions.

1. When did Yannick do his work placement? (1)
2. Where did he work? Mention any two things. (2)
3. What tasks did he have to do? (3)
4. Why did he like the placement? Mention any three things. (3)

Now it's your turn. Write a paragraph about any work experience and/or past job you have had.

CURRENT WORK

You may currently have a job and want to write about this. If you have a job at the moment, use the vocabulary you have just learned but change to the present tense. Refer back to page 7 for this. The only real change for this part will be the time phrases:

- En ce moment
- Depuis un an
- Pendant les vacances
- Tous les week-ends/les soirs

You are now ready to write about any job you currently have. Remember this will be in the present tense, but the vocabulary and phrases will remain the same.

 ONLINE TEST

Take the 'Related work experience' test online at www.brightredbooks.net/N5French

 THINGS TO DO AND THINK ABOUT

You should now have written the first four predictable bullet points. These bullet points will *always* be part of the job application and if you learn them well you should feel comfortable to reproduce what you have written in accurate French.

BULLET POINTS 5 AND 6: THE UNPREDICTABLE ONES

Now let's move onto the two unpredictable bullet points. These will change every year but will still relate to applying for a job. Don't forget the contexts and topics you will have already covered at National 5, as many of these could help you to complete these unpredictable points.

It would be impossible to try to cover every possibility in this book, but below are a few examples.

We will start with the examples given in the sample question paper at the beginning of this section.

WHEN YOU WILL BE AVAILABLE FOR INTERVIEW AND TO WORK?

- Je serai disponible pour un entretien le 5 juin.
- Je pourrais commencer à travailler chez vous à partir du 1er juillet.

ANY LINKS TO BELGIUM OR ANOTHER FRENCH-SPEAKING COUNTRY?

DON'T FORGET

You will have already covered this under the context of culture, so refer back to pages 74–81.

If you were asked to cover this bullet point you may wish to talk about a past trip to a French-speaking country or maybe you visit a French speaking country on a more regular basis as you have family or friends living there.

Here are a couple of examples to give you an idea of what you could write.

1. Il y a deux ans, je suis allé en Belgique pendant une semaine. J'y suis allé avec en groupe scolaire et on a logé dans une auberge de jeunesse. On a visité beaucoup de monuments et de sites touristiques. Je me suis très bien amusé et j'ai amélioré mon français. J'aimerais bien y retourner.

2. Tous les ans, je passe les grandes vacances en France car ma tante habite un petit village pas loin de Lyon. Je passe les journées à faire des promenades ou à me baigner dans sa piscine. J'adore aller en France. La cuisine française est vraiment délicieuse, il fait souvent très beau et j'aime bien parler en français avec les habitants.

OTHER POSSIBILITIES

You may be required to ask questions about something work related, therefore it is really important you know how to form a question in French so you can adapt your question, no matter what it is.

Question words

What do these question words mean?

- Comment?
- Qui?
- Où?

- Pourquoi?
- Quel/quelle/quels/ quelles?

- Que?
- Combien?
- Combien de temps?

To form questions in French you can:

- invert the verb and subject
- use *est-ce que*

- raise your voice at the end of sentence.

ONLINE TEST

Take the 'Unpredictable bullet points' test online at www.brightredbooks.net/ N5French.

contd

As this is a written piece, it would be better to use one of the first two possibilities.

Est-ce que je dois porter un uniforme?	or	Dois-je porter un uniforme?
Est-ce que je serai logé(e)/nourri(e)?	or	Serai-je logé(e)/nourri(e)?
Est-ce que je dois travailler les week-ends et les soirs?	or	Dois-je travailler les week-ends et les soirs?
Est-ce que j'aurai des jours de congés?	or	Aurai-je des jours de congés?
Est-ce qu'il y a une navette/des transports en commun de l'aéroport/de la gare jusqu'à chez vous?		
	or	
Y-a-il une navette/des transports en commun de l'aéroport/de la gare jusqu'à chez vous?		

There may be other unpredictable bullet points that have not been included here. With your teacher/lecturer you will be able to work on some of your own ideas.

You should now have a complete piece of writing.

TOP TIPS

- Always read the job advert thoroughly and apply for the job that is being advertised.
- Write in paragraphs – this will ensure you cover all the bullet points and make it easier for the marker to check your work.
- Write neatly. Markers have to mark a lot of papers and it is really important that they can read your handwriting.
- The first four bullet points will always be the same, so learn these really well.
- Learn how to spell *Je m'appelle* and remember that in French you use avoir with your age. Get off to good start.
- When talking about where you live, remember to use *à* for a village/town/city and *en* for a feminine country: *en Ecosse, en France*.
- Be careful when talking about your subjects. Make sure you spell them correctly.
- Adjectival agreements – think about these carefully. They need to agree in the feminine singular, masculine plural and feminine plural.
- When writing a date the French say, for example, *le 10 mai*. Do not write *10th mai*.
- When writing about a job, do not use *un* or *une*, for example *En ce moment je travaille comme serveur* not *Je travaille comme un serveur*.
- For the final two bullet points, which are less predictable, make sure your French is accurate. Your teacher/lecturer will have covered many possibilities with you so try to learn these.
- Be careful when asking questions. Either use *Est-ce que* or invert the verb and the subject, for example *Est-ce que je dois travailler le week-end?* or *Dois-je travailler le week-end?*
- Remember to *always* read over your work at the end. Check the following:

• Does it make sense?	• Is my spelling accurate?	• Have I agreed adjectives?
• Have I covered all the bullet points?	• Have I used my accents correctly?	• Are my tenses accurate?

- Finally *only* use the dictionary to check spelling/genders/accents. *Do not* try to translate phrases in your head from English to French.

THINGS TO DO AND THINK ABOUT

Here are some top tips to help you learn:

• Make sure your French is accurate – know your grammar points.	• Make sure you fully understand what you are writing.	• Do not start learning the night before.
• To help you learn, read a line, close your jotter and write it out again.	• Change any sentences/phrases you find difficult to remember.	• Have a good revision schedule in place.
• Check over your work.	• Only use a dictionary to check spelling. Do not start making up sentences on the day.	• Always check your written piece.

COURSE ASSESSMENT

The Course assessment at National 5 will take the form of a Performance (talking assessment) and two question papers allowing you to demonstrate your reading, writing and listening skills in French.

PERFORMANCE/TALKING (30 MARKS)

The Performance will allow you to demonstrate your ability to communicate orally in French. After studying the topics at National 5, you will have prepared written pieces of work that should help you with your Performance. The Performance is made up of two parts:

- presentation – 10 marks
- conversation – 20 marks

Presentation

You will be required to give a spoken presentation in French, using detailed language on a topic chosen from one of the following contexts:

- society
- learning
- employability
- culture.

You will choose the topic and develop it into a short presentation of approximately 1½ minutes to allow demonstration of your language skills, accuracy, pronunciation and intonation.

You will be allowed to refer to up to five headings of no more than eight words each as prompts during the presentation and/or use visual aids. The headings may be in French or English.

You teacher/lecturer will listen to your presentation and ask questions based on it in order to engage you in a conversation on the topic.

Conversation

Following the prepared presentation, you will be required to take part in a conversation and to respond to some questions in French following on naturally from the presentation topic chosen.

The conversation should last approximately 4–5 minutes to allow you to demonstrate your ability to take part in a conversation in French using detailed language.

You may refer to other contexts if you wish. The information to be exchanged will be mainly of a factual nature, but will also include some ideas and opinions. You will also ask questions where appropriate.

Within this section marks will be awarded as follows:

- 15 marks for conversation
- 5 marks for effective communication by using natural, detailed language.

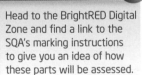

ONLINE

Head to the BrightRED Digital Zone and find a link to the SQA's marking instructions to give you an idea of how these parts will be assessed.

QUESTION PAPER 1 – READING AND WRITING (50 MARKS)

This question paper will assess the skills of reading and writing. The question paper will have two sections:

- reading – 30 marks
- writing – 20 marks

Section 1 (reading)

You will read three texts and demonstrate your understanding by providing answers in English to the questions asked.

Each text will be based on one of the four contexts (society, learning, employability, culture) and all the texts will be of equal length and difficulty.

contd

This section is worth a total of 30 marks, with each text being worth 10 marks. There will be 1–2 supported marks in each text, with one of these total 3–6 supported marks being an overall purpose question.

There will be a variety of question styles and you will be allowed to use a dictionary.

Section 2 (writing)

You will be required to write an email of 120–150 words in French in response to a job advert. There will be four predictable bullet points and two less predictable bullet points. You should have prepared for this thoroughly beforehand and should feel fully equipped to tackle this paper. You will, however, be allowed to use a dictionary.

For help with this section, refer to pages 84–95 of this book.

QUESTION PAPER 2 – LISTENING (20 MARKS)

You will listen to one monologue in French worth 8 marks and one short conversation in French worth 12 marks. You will demonstrate your understanding by providing short answers in English to the questions asked.

This paper will be based on the context which was not covered in Question paper 1, for example if the reading texts cover society, culture and learning then the listening paper will be on employability.

This paper is worth a total of 20 marks and there will be a total of 2–3 supported marks, one of which will be in the monologue and will relate to the speaker's 'intent/reason/attitude/opinion'.

TOP TIPS FOR TACKLING THE EXAM

- If possible, do some practice exam papers beforehand.
- Ensure you go to bed early the night before, having done all of your revision well in advance. If you are tired on the day it will affect your Performance.
- Ensure that your mobile phone is switched off and not kept in your pocket. If your phone goes off during the Course assessment you could be asked to leave the room.
- Make sure you check that you have the right paper in front of you as soon as you sit down. Usually you will be given the correct one but mistakes can be made so don't risk it!

- Read the introduction carefully and use the questions to help lead you to the answer.
- Only use the dictionary if absolutely necessary. The first word you see in the dictionary may not be the one you need so do read all meanings and choose the one that makes the most sense.
- Use *all* the time given and check your answers carefully. Remember, if they do not make sense to you, they will not make sense to the marker. *Check your English too*!

HOW DOES THE SQA ARRIVE AT YOUR FINAL GRADE?

Once you have competed all of your external assessments, each of the marks you achieve will be added together and the examiners will give you an overall mark out of 100 which will translate into your grade. The percentages for achieving each grade vary, but obviously the higher the better!

THINGS TO DO AND THINK ABOUT

Now you should know:
- what is meant by the terms 'Unit assessment' and 'Course assessment'
- what is involved in your Performance
- what is involved in the Reading/Writing paper
- what is involved in the Listening paper

Be sure to make good use of this book and all of your course materials while you prepare for your National 5 assessments – you have the skills and the tools necessary to succeed and as long as you do your best you will achieve a grade of which you can be proud. Stay relaxed and focused and, most of all, bonne chance!

GLOSSARY

adjectives – describe a noun e.g. big – grand; small – petit

adverbs – describe/modify verbs, adjectives and other adverbs e.g. slowly – lentement; quickly – rapidement

avoir phrases – phrases in French which use the verb avoir, e.g. avoir faim – to be hungry

comparatives – the comparison of two or more nouns in terms of more or less, greater or lesser, we normally add 'er' to the end of an adjective or adverb to make the comparison, e.g. John is taller than Brian – John est plus grand que Brian

conditional tense – used to describe what someone would do or what would happen e.g. I would play football – je jouerais au foot

conjunctions – linking words or connectors e.g. and – et; but – mais; however – pourtant

Definite article – 'the' in English; le, la, l', les in French

false friends – a word that looks similar in two languages but means different things in each language e.g. sensible means sensitive in French

imperfect tense – used to describe a past, repeated action, what used to happen, what was happening or what something was like in the past e.g. I used to play/was playing football – je jouais au foot

indefinite article – 'a' or 'an' in English, 'un' or 'une' in French e.g. he has a car – il a une voiture

infinitive – the name/title/basic form of a verb that doesn't specify who is doing the verb (the subject) or when the verb is carried out (tense). In English, the infinitive has the word 'to' infringe of it, e.g. to play; in French the infinitive will end in-er, -ir, -re e.g jouer, finir, vendre

intensifiers – a word that adds force to a verb, adjective or adverb e.g. really – vraiment, too – trop

irregular past participles – verbs in their past form that do not follow the usual pattern e.g. in English when the past part of the verb doesn't end in -ed e.g. seen- vu; done- fait

irregular verbs – verbs that don't follow a regular pattern when they are conjugated (put in different forms in different tenses) e.g. to have – avoir; to be – être

KAL – knowledge about language e.g. vocabulary, grammar, tenses

modal verbs – a verb that combines with another verb to indicate mood, necessity or possibility e.g. to want to – vouloir; to have to – devoir; to be able to – pouvoir

near future tense – used to describe what someone will do or what will happen in the future, e.g. I will play football – je jouerai au foot

negatives – words which negate the verb e.g. I don't play – je ne joue pas; he doesn't like – il n'aime pas; I never go – je ne vais jamais

nouns – name a person, place, thing, quality or action e.g. people – les gens; classroom – la salle de classe; pencil – le crayon

past participle – verbs in their past form. In English we usually add -ed to the end of the verb and in French, we chop off the ending of the verb and for -er verbs, we add é e.g. joué- played; for -ir verbs we add i e.g. fini – finished; and for -re verbs we add -u e.g. repondu – answered

perfect tense – used to describe a past completed action e.g. I (have) played – j'ai joué

prepositions – a word that indicates the relationship between a noun or pronoun and other words in a sentence e.g. the book is on the table – le livre est sur la table

present tense – used to describe what usually happens or what is happening in the present e.g. I eat/ I am eating – je mange

Pronoun – a word that takes the place of a noun e.g. John eats chocolate can be changed to 'he eats it'

reflexive verbs – verbs that are done to oneself e.g. to wash oneself – se laver; I wash myself – je me lave

regular verbs – verbs that follow a pattern when conjugated (put in different forms in different tenses) e.g. to play – jouer

relative pronouns – used to link what is stated in different clauses e.g. who, what, which, what, whom, where, when. I have a dog who is called Max – j'ai un chien qui s'appelle Max

simple future tense – used to describe what is going to happen or what someone is going to do in the future e.g. I am going to play football – je vais jouer au foot

subject pronouns – the person or thing that does the verb e.g. I – je; you – tu; he – il; she – elle etc.

superlatives – used in comparisons to show which noun is the most or least of a quality or characteristic e.g. the tallest – le plus grand

tense – indicates when the verb takes place (present/ past/future)

Verbs – action words e.g. I play football – je joue au foot (play is the verb)